THE INSIDE PASSAGE TO ALASKA

A SHORT HISTORY

by Hugo Anderson

Cover & Illustrations by Hugo Anderson III

First Edition July, 1998. Printed in U.S.A. ISBN 0-945989-21-0

1

THE INSIDE PASSAGE
Washington & British Columbia

BRITISH
COLUMBIA

Nootka
Sound

Vancouver Island

Vancouver

Fraser
River

CANADA

Pacific
Ocean

Victoria

Bellingham

Juan de Fuca Strait

UNITED STATES

WASHINGTON

Seattle

Olympia

N

THE INSIDE PASSAGE
British Columbia and Southeast Alaska

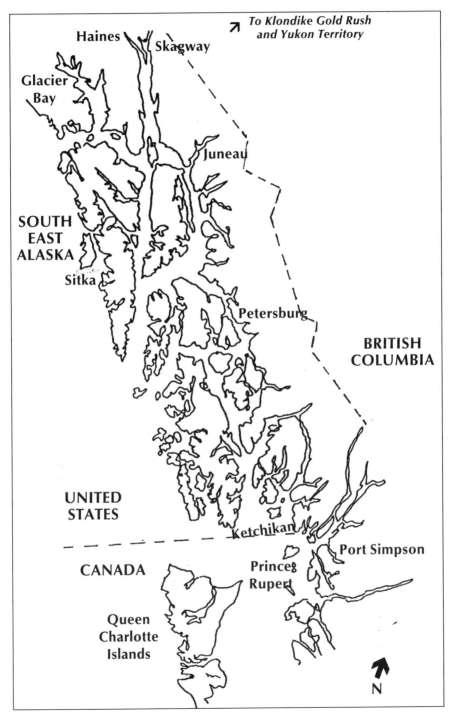

To Klondike Gold Rush
and Yukon Territory

Haines

Skagway

Glacier
Bay

Juneau

SOUTH
EAST
ALASKA

Sitka

Petersburg

BRITISH
COLUMBIA

UNITED
STATES

Ketchikan

Port Simpson

CANADA

Prince
Rupert

Queen
Charlotte
Islands

N

The restored Russian Bishop's House, originally built in Sitka in 1842, is the oldest intact Russian building. It was the site of the transfer of Alaska from Russian to United States ownership.

Furnishings in the Russian Bishop's House include church altars and artifacts.

TABLE OF CONTENTS

Many times people appear reluctant to delve into history books, even those containing extremely interesting history, because of the mass of documents and details involved. In writing this book, I have tried to capture the significance, excitement, and importance of the Inside Passage, and to do it as briefly and concisely as possible. In addition to descriptions of the physical attributes of the region, the first inhabitants, and explorers; emphasis has also been placed on natural resources and associated industries, and how they have shaped the history of the area.

FOREWORD

Researching the information has taken several years. My first hand knowledge began with camping excursions in the 1930's, car and trailer trips on Vancouver Island during the years through the 1970's, visiting Alaska Marine Highway ports-of-call on board the Alaska ferry, and finally, cruising the Inside Passage in the 1980's and 1990's on board our own 34' boat, the *Sea Otter*. Eleven times we have boated as far north as Prince Rupert, British Columbia, and five times have continued north in Alaskan waters to Glacier Bay and Skagway. While on our adventures, we explored the cities, towns, and villages, visited museums and historical sites.

The one thousand miles of protected, scenic waterways from Olympia, Washington to Skagway, Alaska constitute the so-called "Inside Passage", and are the best cruising waters in the world, whether by small boat, ferry, or large modern cruise ship. In 1879, John Muir, the famous naturalist and the first European to explore Glacier Bay, said "Never before this had I been embosomed in scenery so hopelessly beyond description, tracing shining ways through fjord and sound, past forests and waterfalls, islands and mountains and far azure headlands, it seems as if surely we must at length reach the very paradise of the poets, the abode of the blessed." It would be difficult to improve on Muir's words, and the beauty he saw in 1879 is largely unchanged to this day. Although Muir was describing Southeast Alaska, the author believes Muir's words apply to the entire Inside Passage.

CHAPTER ONE

THE INSIDE PASSAGE

ITS FORMATION

When travelling the 1,100 mile Inside Passage from Washington State, along the British Columbia coast to Alaska, it is hard not to wonder how the mountains, islands and waterways through which you are passing were created. Geographically the Northwest Coast is divided lengthwise into three areas, (1) the mainland mountains to the east, (2) the Coastal Trough, containing the "Inside Passage", extending northwest from Puget Sound and (3) to the west, the Insular Mountains consisting of Vancouver Island, the Queen Charlotte Islands, and the mountains of the Alexander Archipelago in Southeast Alaska. These offshore islands are a mountain range that was "drowned" when the ocean rose as the ice cap melted at the end of the last ice age.

In the 1960's geologists began to theorize that such formations were created by the movement of what they called tectonic plates. These tectonic plates are independent, rigid sections of the earth's crust, six to twenty miles thick, that float on earth's molten magma core, and are in motion. In this region the Pacific Plate has been moving east, colliding with the western North American Plate. Since the Pacific Plate is composed of denser, heavier rock from the ocean floor, it is forced under the lighter rocks of the North American Plate, and is then absorbed back into the hot mantle of the earth from which it originally came. The force of this collision millions of years ago buckled and pushed up the rocks of the North American Plate, creating mountains, and depressions, and the numerous volcanoes from Mount Lassen in California, north and west, up the coast, through the Aleutian Chain in Alaska.

These volcanoes occur when the molten magma of the earth's core breaks through a weak spot in the surface of the earth, and lava pours out, gradually building up huge mountains. Evidence of past volcanic activity is present all along the northwest coast of North America in the form of extinct, or dormant volcanoes, such as Mount Hood, in Oregon and Mount Rainier and Mount Baker, as well as recently active Mount Saint Helens in Washington state. The pressures caused by plate movements are also the cause of the numerous earthquakes in this region, the largest of recent record being the Great Alaskan Earthquake of 1964.

There is evidence of volcanic activity of fairly recent origin, since the last Ice Age, in the form of volcanic cinder cones that were not disturbed by the ice. One such cone is clearly visible in daylight from the B. C. Ferry, or from any other ship, when passing, is an 800 foot cone on the south end of Swindle Island, near the village of Klemtu. Much more recent are lava flows in the Nass River valley of northern British Columbia, just south of the Alaskan border. These lava beds are thought to be no more than 300 years old, and the time of formation is remembered in Indian tribal history. Other evidence of seismic activity is the number of hot springs along the coast in both Alaska and British Columbia.

The entire Pacific Coast, and most of the western mountains, consist of some 50 different pieces of the earth's surface which emigrated from other positions on earth. Large islands and small continents piled up against the western edge of North America, and stuck there as the surrounding ocean floor, which had carried them there, disappeared back into earth's core. Some of these rocks can be found in mountains 300 miles to the east of the present coast line.

Though the mountain ranges and the Coastal Trough were originally formed by tectonic plate movement and volcanism, the finished product that we see today is the work of the glaciers of the last Ice Age. This is still continuing today.

A glacier is formed on land in those areas where more snow crystals accumulate annually than melt. Over many years the accumulation becomes deep enough to form glacial ice, which, because of it's own weight and through the influence of gravity, begins to flow. To be defined as a glacier the ice mass must move, or "flow". A glacier is best described as a "river of ice". It flows like a river, but very slowly. As it flows, a glacier picks up rocks and large boulders in its sole, or bottom, from the rocks over which it flows. The sides of the glacier also pick up boulders from the valley walls. It is these boulders, embedded in the glacial ice, that provide the scouring action that erodes the rocks over which it passes. The ice itself is much softer, and erosion from it alone would be much slower. If the terrain is fairly flat, as in northern Ontario, the glaciers will scour off softer sedimentary rock until they reach the hard granite bedrock as they did when they created the thousand mile wide Canadian Shield. If the glaciers flow over previously created mountain ridges and valleys, as they have along the northwest coast of North America, gravity will set their courses down the valleys, which they will cut even deeper. The proof of this scouring action by glacial boulders can be seen along the walls of many of the fiords that lead into the Inside Passage, as well as along the walls of the passage itself.

Glacial valleys in the mountains that have not been filled with sea water can easily be recognized by their U shape, where the glacier formerly rested on the relatively flat bottom. In contrast, stream cut mountain valleys are V shaped as the stream cuts ever deeper into the bottom of the valley. The heads of most glacial valleys end in a bowl shape called a cirque, where the glacier remnant melted.

Where glacial boulders have cut into these walls they cut grooves, or striations, that can still be seen. Most of this action takes place in the sole of the glacier, where the tremendous weight of the glacier results in more rapid erosion. These areas are not as visible because they are either covered by water in the fiords or lakes, or by subsequent plant growth in the mountains.

As a glacier flows, it moves over irregularities in the valley floor which cause it to bend. These bends and friction between the sides of the glacier and valley walls, cause large cracks, called crevasses, to appear in the ice body of the glacier. All true glaciers, as compared to snow fields, have some crevasses in them.

If a glacier is always moving, a good question is "Where is it going?" The answer is "down", until it reaches a climate warm enough to cause it to melt. If the amount of melting each year equals the amount of new snow falling on the snow field at its head, the glacier is said to be "stationary." If the snowfall exceeds the melt, the glacier will be "advancing." If it is less, the glacier will be "retreating." The glaciers of the Coast Range are remnants of the last Ice Age, and at present most of them are retreating, though Taku glacier, south of Juneau, and the glaciers of the Fairweather Mountain Range, on the west side of Glacier Bay National Park, are advancing. Though there are glaciers to be seen in the mountains all along the Inside Passage, they only reach the salt water, to become "tide-water glaciers" in three places, all of which are in Alaska. These are in Glacier Bay National Park, Holkham Bay south of Juneau, and in LeConte Bay near Petersburg.

Most people live in areas remote from glaciers, and, therefore are not familiar with them. They are not rare, however. In fact, ice covers ten percent of the globe. Glaciers and polar ice caps contain more fresh water than lakes, rivers, ground water and the atmosphere combined. No wonder scientists become concerned when they discuss the "greenhouse effect" and its possible influence on increasing the amount of melting ice.

The glaciers that we see today along the west coast are remnants of the last of several continental ice sheets that created the so called "Ice Ages" of the Pliestocene Epoch, from 10,000 to 1,800,000 years ago. They covered most of northern North America, as well as northern Europe and Asia.

Erosion was not the only effect that these ice sheets had on the land masses. As the amount of water contained in the ice sheets increased, the water contained in the oceans became less and the result was a dramatic drop in sea level. On the other hand the tremendous weight of the ice, over a mile thick, resulted in compression of the rocks, thereby lowering the level of the land. Over a long period of time, the level of the sea experienced wide fluctuations, alternately exposing and flooding large areas of land. About 10,000 years ago, with the last retreat of the ice, sea level has risen, flooding the valleys we see as inlets and fiords today.

In Glacier Bay National Park, which was filled with ice 4,000 to 5,000 feet thick as recently as 200 years ago, the land is still "rebounding" from the effect, as much as a foot in just over eight years in the Beardslee Islands. Ice 4,000 feet thick would exert a pressure on the land of more than three million tons per square mile.

CLIMATE

It is difficult characterizing the climate for a region one thousand miles long, with its wide local variations as well. In general, in spite of its northerly location, the Inside Passage has a relatively mild, wet marine climate. Seattle is about the same latitude as northern Maine and Minnesota, and Juneau is even with Hudson's Bay. The cause of the relatively mild climate is the adjacent warm Pacific Ocean, and the prevailing westerly winds which cross it.

Summers are mild, very hot weather is rare, and winters are cool, but not severely cold; subzero temperatures, even in the Alaskan section of the Inside Passage are rare. The Inside Passage remains ice free for its entire length all year long. Storms are most frequent and precipitation is heaviest from November through January. Long periods of rain and drizzle are common in the winter, and summers can have long periods of warm sunny days. Annual precipitation ranges from an average of 154 inches in Ketchikan to 26 inches in Skagway, 27 inches in Victoria on Vancouver Island, and 35 inches in Seattle.

Needless to say, the climate has been a most important factor in the development of the Inside Passage. The mild temperatures allowed the use of the thousand mile long *Marine Highway*, first by the native population and today by thousands of tourists. It is also an important trade artery. The wet climate encouraged the growth of tremendous forests along the entire length of the passage and made possible the forestry industry that is so important to the area. This same wet climate also created the numerous rivers, large and small, that are the spawning grounds of salmon. Salmon fishing, both commercial and sport, and their support industries such as canneries and boat building, are important industries. The forests also were the habitat of some of the various fur-bearing animals, the resource that brought the first Europeans to this area.

THE SEA

The sea created the mild wet climate that gave this region its biggest asset, the plant and animal life. The salt water was also the reason that the first humans came to this region. They came from the interior, after previously arriving from Asia. They came down the river valleys and found in abundance the requisites for living, food, shelter and a mild climate. Eventually they populated the entire northwest coast and all of North, Central and South America.

All of the oceans of the earth are subject to diurnal, twice daily, tidal fluctuations caused by the gravitational pull of both the sun and the moon. These tidal changes create currents that can be very strong especially in areas such as the northwest coast where the numerous islands and inlets create narrow waterways which restrict the tidal flows, resulting in very strong currents as the sea pushes through the narrow passages. Another characteristic of tides is that fluctuations are the least near the equator and generally increase towards higher latitudes. To the first inhabitants, the tidal fluctuations were important, as low tides uncovered the shellfish and crustaceans and various sea weeds that were very important sources of food. An old native saying was that "when the tide is out, the table is set".

Tidal ranges and currents vary widely at different times in their monthly cycle. The biggest tides, called "spring tides" and the fastest currents occur when the sun and moon are aligned. The least tides, "neap tides" and slowest currents occur when they are opposed. These maximums and minimums occur twice each month.

Tide and Current Tables are published for waters all over the world, giving the time and height of the high and low tides for each day for thousands of locations. For currents, the tables give the times of current changes, at "slack tide" and the time and velocity when maximum currents occur.

FLORA

Because of the mild, wet climate along the Inside Passage, plant life on land has flourished. Dense forests predominate, covering the mountain-sides right down to the waters edge. A passerby may notice that the trees along the shoreline have their lower limbs sheared off so evenly that they appear to have been trimmed by a gardener. This is the work of salt spray during times of high tides and storms. The spray kills the growth on the lower limbs, keeping them trimmed. If you were to go ashore and attempt to walk into the forest, you would find it difficult or impossible to go very far. It is a true jungle of trees, fallen trees, and underbrush.

Most of the trees are coniferous, or evergreen. Western Hemlock, Sitka Spruce, Douglas Fir, and Red Cedar predominate. Alders are the most common deciduous trees, and in the far southern section of the passage there are maple, oak, some arbutus and dogwood; the latter is the provincial tree and flower of the Province of British Columbia.

The sea also contains an abundance of plant life. Shallow areas are covered with eelgrass, a favorite cover for crabs and other forms of life, and a source of food for geese. There are various types of algae or sea weed, the largest of which are the kelp which can attain lengths of 80 to 100 feet.

FAUNA

Animal life is plentiful along the Inside Passage, both on shore and in the sea, but especially in the latter. The land animals are predominantly mammals, birds and insects. Among the mammals are Columbia Black Tail Deer, a coastal relative of the mule deer of the interior, Black Bear with color variations of Cinnamon, Blue and the very rare white or Kermode Bear of Northern British Columbia, and the Grizzly Bear. The Alaskan Brown Bear, now recognized as a type of Grizzly, is also found in northern sections. Mountain Goats and Gray Wolves are also present. The weasel family is represented by weasels, mink, marten, fisher, wolverine and two kinds of otter; sea otters and smaller river otters. Foxes, raccoons and squirrels are also found, as well as smaller mammals such as mice, voles and shrews. Although the forests are rich in mammalian life, that is usually not evident to waterborne travellers because of the denseness of the forest cover.

Aquatic mammals include four species of whales; Orca or Killer

Whale, Humpback, Gray and Minke, as well as Dall and Harbor Porpoises, Harbor and Elephant Seals, Steller and California Sea Lions and the Sea Otter.

Many species of land birds are also to be found in the woodlands and along the shore, including the Bald Eagle, Osprey, Peregrine Falcon, grouse, crows, ravens, woodpeckers and numerous song birds.

Seashore birds are, by far, the most obvious form of animal life seen along the Inside Passage. Indeed, it is rare when some bird or birds are not in sight. The gulls are most numerous, with the large glaucous winged gull being the most common species. Others are the small Bonaparte Gulls and the middle-sized Ring-Billed Gulls. In late summer, several Tern species are seen as well as Storm Petrels and Sooty Shearwaters. Large flocks of Common and Surf Scoters fly in string formations just above the water. Several kinds of ducks are found including Barrows and Common Goldeneyes and the shy, beautiful Harlequin Duck along with Canada and Snow Geese, and their smaller cousins the Brant. The very large white Trumpeter Swans are seen along the shorelines as are Blue Herons, Sandhill Cranes, several species of Sandpipers, Yellowlegs and noisy Black Oystercatchers. There are three species of Loons, which can often be heard uttering their eerie cries, and large rafts of Western Grebes are occasionally seen. Cormorants are common in southern sections.

Members of the Alcid family are also very common. They are the Common Murre, Pigeon Guillemot, Tufted Puffin, Auklets and Murrelets. They are unusual in that they come ashore only to breed, and that they use their wings when swimming underwater as well as when flying. Except for the brown, robin-sized murrelets both sexes are black and white.

If birds seem to be everywhere, it is the underwater world that really teems with animal life along the Inside Passage. This is obvious from the activities of the sea birds pursuing fish as well as the numerous sport and commercial fishing activities. Of all of the fish the five species of Pacific Salmon, (Chinook, Coho, Sockeye, Pink and Chum) are the best known and the most sought after. The taking and preparation of salmon is one of the major industries of the northwest coast.

Herring is the second most valuable commercial species in these waters, as well as a principle source of food for many of the larger species, especially the salmon. It is taken primarily for its roe, which is marketed in Japan. The rest of the fish is rendered for fertilizer. The Pacific Halibut is another very popular fish with both commercial and sport fishermen. It is a big flat bottom-dwelling fish that can exceed 500 pounds in weight, though most are smaller, from 20 to 80 pounds. Other common fish are several species of rockfish, cod, (both true cod and black cod), Greenling and Lingcod. Shark are also found in these waters, especially the small, three to four foot sandshark, commonly called Dogfish. Larger sharks, like the six-gilled shark are here, but seldom seen as they prefer the deep water. Other important forms of undersea animal life are the shellfish, such as scallops and prawns. Dungeness, Rock and King Crab, are prevalent, the latter only in northern waters. Mussels, oysters, abalone, and various types of clams are also found as are Sea Urchins, starfish, anemones, barnacles, jellyfish and corals. The largest octopi in the world inhabit these waters, but because of their shy nature they are seldom seen, except by divers.

To this point in this *Inside Passage Story*, the descriptions have dealt with the natural features of the land, sea and nonhuman fauna and flora. In the recent past man has carved the region into three political divisions, the states of Alaska and Washington of the United States, with the Canadian Province of British Columbia lying between them. The total distance from Olympia, Washington to Skagway, Alaska, is about 1,100 nautical miles, or about 1,250 statute miles. Of this total distance 145 miles are in Washington, 575 miles in British Columbia, and 350 miles in Alaska, all nautical miles. This totals 575 miles in Canadian waters and 525 in United States waters, or about half and half.

New Eddystone Rock, a volcanic plug, is found in Behm Canal near Ketchikan.

14

CHAPTER TWO

THE FIRST INHABITANTS

In any discussion of the natives of the North Pacific mainland and islands, the starting point should be, "Where did they come from?" and "How did they get there?"

It is still generally accepted that men first came to North and South America from Siberia about 12,000 years ago, or earlier, by crossing the Bering Strait on a land bridge that existed towards the end of the last Great Ice Age. Some anthropologists believe that this was not the first migration to occur, that earlier ones, also from Siberia, had previously crossed land bridges to North America. Recent finds of human remains or artifacts support this idea. Along with this theory goes the belief that these earlier migrants had continued south, perhaps in an opening between the Ice Caps, and that they later returned north as the glaciers retreated.

Oral histories of the coast tribes state that their ancestors had come from the south, not the north, and reached the coast by way of several of the large river valleys, such as the Fraser, Skeena, Stikine, Columbia, Taku, Nass, and Bella Coola. When they reached the coast, they found what they were looking for, a land with many advantages. Primarily it had food, not merely enough to get by on, but a large surplus, which was very easy to gather. There were also dense forests that had cedar, among other trees. The cedar provided them with wood for shelter and the building of canoes for transportation. The fibers also furnished raw materials for garments and basket weaving. The waters of the rivers and ocean provided an easy means of transportation. The climate, though wet, was moderate, which made survival easier. Why search any farther? They settled down.

Proof that the first inhabitants of North America came from Siberia is found in the common traits in the culture and physical characteristics of the natives of northeastern Siberia and the natives of Northwestern North America. A recent large display exhibited in Seattle through the joint efforts of the United States and Russian governments emphasized these facts very clearly.

The dry interior plains of Alaska and the Yukon were not glaciated in the Last Ice Age, and fossilized remains of horses, camels, deer, caribou, and even mammoths, species now largely extinct in North America, tell of animals that would have been a source of food for nomads from Asia as they moved east and south through that area.

Once they reached the coast the new inhabitants settled on the shore, or on river banks, as this was where the sources of food were located. The natives of the Northwest Coast did not have to roam large areas of land searching for their food, and live a nomadic life as did the tribes of the interior and plains. Instead the food was either right in front of them, or came to them in the forms of the migrating salmon.

Salmon was the most important food, taken by weirs and traps placed in the rivers and streams when the salmon migrated annually to their spawning grounds. They were salted and smoked, providing a surplus of food. Oolichan, or candlefish, were also taken by the same method, and were primarily rendered in heated wooden vessels, by placing hot stones in them. The oil was considered a delicacy. Shellfish, primarily mussels and clams, were another important source of food, as is evident by the numerous "kitchen middens" along the Inside Passage. The middens look like white sand beaches, but are really broken shells that have accumulated over thousands of years in front of the native villages and camps along the coast line. Accumulations may be as deep as 15 to 20 feet in some places; all life focused on the beach. Halibut were also taken, using wood and bone hooks, bait, and rocks for weights. Some tribes engaged in whaling, notably the Haidas and Nootkas in British Columbia, and the Makahs from the Olympic Peninsula in Washington. Whales were taken from large cedar canoes, with spears. Just inside the entrance to the Royal British Columbia Museum in Victoria, British Columbia, is an excellent diorama depicting how this was done. Sea mammals such as seals, sea lions, dolphins and sea otter also were taken from the canoes.

Surplus food supplies, smoked salmon, and oolichan oil, were traded with tribes from the interior. The trails that were used were called "grease trails."

Despite the lack of agriculture, the tribes of the northern coastal regions were the most complex culturally, just prior to the arrival of Europeans, having the greatest population density in native North America.

Winter villages consisted of great plank houses, with huge support poles and rafters from whole cedar logs. They faced the beach, often fortified or placed on protected points of land, for protection from raiding parties. The planks were split from cedar logs with stone

16

and bone tools. Fishing stations and summer camps were placed in good fishing locations, primarily up rivers and streams where the salmon migrated. These were only *temporary camps.*

Travel was by water along the coastline, or up rivers, in dugout canoes, both large and small, created from cedar logs. The large craft could be up to 30 feet in length, and could carry a large party of people.

Native Northwest Coast art style was highly symbolic. The totem poles, or family crests, marking the villages, are probably the best known examples of their art style. Wood implements, primarily of cedar, were often ornamented by carving, painting, and inlaid shells. The entrances of their large houses were similarly decorated. Basket weaving was another form of utilitarian art. The baskets were so tightly woven that they would hold water, and were used for cooking by placing hot stones in them. If you are interested in Northwest Coast art the largest collections are in the Museum of Anthropology at the University of British Columbia in Vancouver, or the aforementioned Royal British Columbia Museum in Victoria, British Columbia, as well as in several other communities along the Inside Passage.

Organization was by independent villages, not tribally. Class distinctions were emphasized, chiefs and nobles at the top, then commoners, and last, slaves who were prisoners of war. All rank depended on wealth. There was private ownership of land, fishing stations, houses, masks, crests, etc.

Potlatches were an important part of the culture, when chiefs competed in displays of wealth through gifts of property to those in attendance. The greater the amount of the gifts, the greater the status that the donor achieved. These "gifts" were expected to be returned by the recipients through later potlatches.

Religion held an important place in the culture. The winter season had elaborate ceremonies performed by the various societies in a village. The shaman, or medicine man, was an important person in a village.

Warfare between villages, or tribes, was common. It was usually in revenge for earlier slayings, to retrieve lost property, or to take slaves.

The impact on this culture from the arrival of the Europeans, Russians coming from the north (1741), the Spanish from the south (1774), the English (1778), the French (1785) and Americans (1788) also from the south, caused the eventual shattering of tribal life as it had existed. The most important change was the introduction of new diseases of which small pox was the most devastating, largely decimating the population. The Haidas were hit the hardest, as their numbers dropped from about 8,000 to 800. Almost as devastating, and of much longer lasting consequences, was the introduction of alcohol to the natives, primarily by the independent fur traders and, of course bootleggers. The Russian American Company, the Hudson's Bay Company and the American government forbade its sale, but it was always available from some sources. This scourge of the native population still is probably the biggest problem that they face. They seem much more susceptible to succumbing to alcoholism than do the nonnative population.

The relationship between the natives and the newcomers varied widely from tribe to tribe and the types of Europeans involved. In general, it can be said that the European explorers, representatives of their respective governments, whether they were Russian, Spanish, French, or British, treated the natives quite humanely, but the private fur traders were usually very brutal, beginning with the first Russian *promyshlenniki*, who massacred many of the Aleut men, to the British and American fur traders who arrived later.

On the native side, the Tlingits were always the most warlike and bloodthirsty, from their first encounter with Chirikov in 1741, when they killed 18 members of his crew who went ashore for water and wood, down to the killing of United States Customs collector Colonel Isaac Ebey on Whidbey Island, Washington on August 11, 1857. The murderers of Ebey were Tlingits from the village of Kake, Russian America, who paddled that whole distance (about 900 miles) to kill and then behead Colonel Ebey in revenge, it is thought, for the killing of one of their chiefs by the shells from a United States gunboat. Their culture demanded the death of a chief for a slain chief of theirs. Two years later Captain Dodd of the Hudson's Bay Company ship, *LaBouchere*, with considerable risk to himself and his ship and crew, was able to recover the skull and return it to the Ebey family. On the other hand, the Haidas, though the scourge of other native tribes, and the Nootkas in most cases, were known to not only be friendly to the Europeans, but hospitable, inviting them to their homes. Even the friendly tribes had trouble with the fur traders, however, and blood was shed on both sides. When conflicts occurred they were usually one-sided as the Europeans were always better armed, often with the heavy cannon from their ships. This was not always the case, as we shall see later, when the Tlingits massacred the inhabitants of Sitka.

The native population of the northwest coast is not one homogenous group, but is made up of at least nine tribes with distinct linguistic differences. From south to north are found I) Coast Salish (there are also Inland Salish) on the southern mainland of British Columbia on southeast Vancouver Island and in the Puget Sound area of Washington State, 2) Makah on the Olympic Peninsula of Washington, 3) Nootka, on the west coast of Vancouver Island, 4) Kwakiutl on northern Vancouver Island and the central British Columbia Coast, 5) Bella Coola in the valley of the same name, who speak the Salish language, 6) Tsimshian in the area around Prince Rupert, and north to the Alaskan border, 7) Haida in the Queen Charlotte Islands of British Columbia and on islands in southern Alaska, 8) Nishga, in the Nass River area on the British Columbia/Alaska border, 9) Tlingit (pronounced Klinkit) in all of the rest of southeast Alaska.

An entirely different group of natives are the Aleuts of the Aleutian Island chain in Alaska. Though remote from the Inside Passage, they were influential in the period when Europeans first came to the Northwest Pacific because they were employed by the Russians in their sea otter hunting expeditions. On sea otter hunts hundreds of the Aleuts travelled as far south as California in their two man skin biadarkas, led by the Russians in their sailing ships.

Even though these different coastal tribes have their own languages and fought with each other, they share many common characteristics. First, they dwell at the waters edge, and derive most of their food from the animal and plant life of the sea and seashore. Second, they are not nomadic but remain in the area around their permanent villages, though they usually migrate short distances in the summer to fishing camps. Third, their only means of transportation is by water in cedar canoes of all sizes. Fourth, their religions are all similar, being "shamanism" or dominated by so called "medicine men." These shamans are also responsible for preserving and "handing down" their oral histories, since there are no written histories.

Ruins at Mamalilaculla, an abandoned Indian village, and site of the last big Potlatch in 1921.

CHAPTER THREE

EXPLORATION

Until the middle of the eighteenth century, the North Pacific Ocean had not been visited by European explorers, although, by that time, most of the rest of the world's oceans were known. The reason, of course, was the distance from Europe. It was necessary, if going east, to first sail around Africa and Asia, and if going west, around North and South America. In addition, the Spanish who had settlements on the North and South American Pacific Coasts, as well as in the Philippine Islands, considered the Pacific their own private "lake", and did not encourage encroachment by others. This was all to change, beginning in 1728 and later in 1741.

Of all of the explorers who were involved in North Pacific exploration, five stand out: Two Russians, Vitus Bering and Alexander Baranof; two Englishmen, Captains James Cook and George Vancouver; and a Spanish naval officer, Juan Francisco de Bodega y Quadra.

THE RUSSIANS

The first Europeans to investigate Northwest America came not from the east, as had all previous explorers of America, but from the west. They were Russians who sailed from northeastern Siberia, across some of the roughest water on earth, the Bering Sea and the Gulf of Alaska as they are now known. The first explorer was Commander Vitus Bering, a Danish sailor employed by the Russian navy. He was sent by the Czar, Peter the Great, who wrote out his instructions himself, his last official act, as he died soon after that. In July 1728, Bering sailed east and north from Petropavlovsk, a base built by Bering, on the Kamchatka Peninsula of Siberia. On August 8th, during a two month trip, he discovered St. Lawrence Island, about 150 miles off the northwest coast of Alaska. He also determined that Asia was separated by water, the Bering Strait, from whatever land lay to the east. It was another 13 years before Bering set out on his second, and last, trip to Alaskan waters. In June of 1741, he sailed in two 88 foot long two-masted square-rigged ships that were built in Petropavlovsk. Bering was in the *Saint Peter*, and the *Saint Paul* was commanded by Captain-Lieutenant Aleksei Chirikov. They set out on a southeasterly course, but were soon separated in the rain and fog and were forced to go each on his own way. On July 16, 1741, Bering found the mainland of North America in the huge peaks of a mountain range that he named St. Elias in honor of the saint whose day it was. But he did not go ashore.

On the day before, July 15, Chirikov sighted land 400 miles to the southeast. Three days later, off what is believed to have been Prince of Wales Island in southeast Alaska, he sent a boat ashore with eleven armed men to look for water. They were the first white men known to have set foot in Alaska, and also the first to meet the warlike Tlingit natives. When they did not return in five days Chirikov sent a second boat with two men, but they did not return either. After waiting for several more days, he set sail for Petropavlovsk, where, among other things, he reported that the waters all along the coast were full of sea otters and the land populated by unfriendly natives.

Bering and the *Saint Peter*, however, did not return. They were wrecked on a large island off the Kamchatka Peninsula of Siberia when they sought shelter from a storm. They were forced to spend the winter on the island, later named for Bering. Bering died on December 8, 1741, and most of the crew, already sick from scurvy, did not survive either. Those who did survive built a small boat from the remains of the wreck, and were able to reach Petropavlovsk the next summer. In addition to the furs that they wore, they had many more skins of blue fox, fur seals, and most exciting, sea otter. The traders in Petropavlovsk and Okhotsk became very excited about the news of plentiful sea otters in the seas to the east, because they knew that there was a great demand for these furs in China and in Europe where they would bring unbelievably high prices.

After the return of the Bering/Chirikov expeditions, the Russian government lost interest in spending more money and effort on lands so remote. It was over 9,000 miles from the capital, St. Petersburg, to the land found by these two explorers. It was six thousand miles across Russia and Siberia just to reach Okhotsk and the salt water. That part of the trip took from a year to a year and a half, then it was another three thousand miles across some of the roughest water in the world in craft ill suited for those conditions. Russia didn't want the news to reach other European nations, especially the Spaniards who were already in the Pacific, and thought that the ocean was their private domain. To reinforce the Spanish claims there was the Papal Bull of 1493, issued by Pope Alexander VI who divided the "unknown parts of the earth" between the Spaniards and the Portugese. The Spaniards got the Pacific, and wanted to keep it to themselves. They had already moved up the west coast of Mexico into California. There were political "leaks" in those days as there are today, and the Spanish Ambassador to St. Petersburg picked it up and forwarded it to Spain. As we shall soon see this caused quite a stir in the Spanish court.

If the Russian government in St. Petersburg was not interested in further exploration of Alaskan waters, there were men who were very willing to do so. These were the independent fur trappers and traders known as "promyshlenniki". They were descendants of the traders who in 60 years, from 1579 to 1639, had explored all of Siberia, from the Urals to the Pacific, trapping for furs and setting up forts as they progressed. Having seriously depleted the Siberian forests of fur-bearing animals, they were looking for new sources of furs when the expeditions of Bering and Chirikov returned with furs of fox, fur seal and especially sea otter. After trapping on the islands near the Siberian coast with great success, the first expedition to Alaska set out on September 25, 1745. Since their experience with ships had been limited to river craft, this was the type of ship that they built. These "shitiks", as they were known, were flat bottomed, square-bowed scows with a pair of square-rigged sails. Since iron was not available locally, they used leather thongs to hold their green timbered craft together. Setting out to cross the Gulf of Alaska in such craft, with inexperienced crews, may seem tantamount to suicide, but it did not deter these men. After their experiences in Siberia, they were very accustomed to danger and hardship. Doubtless, many of those who attempted these voyages did not return.

The 1745 voyage by two traders, Chebaevskoi and Trapeznikov, was made with a crew of 60 promyshlenniki under the command of Yakov Choprov. With fair weather and a following wind they reached the Aleutian island of Attu in just six days. They beached their flat bottomed craft and spent a year on Attu. Returning to Siberia in September 1746, they had constant head winds, and, after six weeks, their ship was wrecked on an island off the Kamchatka Peninsula of Siberia. Though 12 lives were lost, as well as all but 300 of their sea otter pelts, the trip was considered a big success, and the rush for the Aleutians was on. It took 18 more years before the Russians sailed the entire 1200 mile length of the Aleutian chain. This was accomplished in 1763 when the island of Kodiak was first sighted. The distance from Okhotsk, on the Siberian mainland was 2700 miles and the total from St. Petersburg almost 9,000 miles.

Even though some improvements had been made in shipbuilding, the so-called *"navigators"* had only the compass and telescope for instruments, and were unable to determine their position when out of sight of land. It should not be surprising then that the progress of exploration was very slow, though the fur trappers were very active on the outer Aleutians. It was not until July of 1784, that a three ship expedition, financed and commanded by the trader Gregory Shelekhov and his wife, Natalie, established a permanent colony at Three Saints Bay, Kodiak Island. The closest European settlement was the tiny Spanish Presidio at San Francisco, 2,000 miles to the southeast.

THE SPANISH

In the meantime, the Spaniards had not been idle in investigating this intrusion into what, as previously mentioned, they considered to be their territory. Accordingly, the frigate *Santiago*, a small ship, was dispatched to the North Pacific from Monterey, California, in June 1774, under the command of Juan Perez. His instructions were to sail to latitude 60 degrees N, to land and take possession of the territory in the name of the King of Spain, Carlos III. This would have been in the Prince William Sound, Alaska area. On July 18th, at 51 degrees, 42 minutes, they sighted land through fog and rain. They were off the Queen Charlotte Islands, in what is now British Columbia, Canada. They needed fresh water, so sailed on northward looking for a place to land. Natives came out from the shore in canoes, and some trading was done with them, but the Spaniards did not go ashore. Perez continued north along the shore of the Queen Charlotte Islands until he reached Langara Island at the northwest corner of the islands. He waited for four days for a favorable wind that would carry him into Dixon Entrance, that today separates Alaska from British Columbia. None came. Many Indians came out in numerous canoes, and trading of trinkets for furs was carried on, but again no one went ashore, though two natives boarded the frigate, and two of the sailors went down into the canoes where they were well received by the friendly Haidas. On July 23rd, Perez gave up and turned south. On August 8th, the *Santiago* sailed into Nootka Sound on Vancouver Island and found the natives to be much less friendly, at least at first, than the Haidas. Only nine men came out in three small canoes and motioned that the ship should leave. In the evening more natives came making mournful sounds and indicating that the Spaniards should leave. Many years later, another Spanish explorer was told that the reason the natives had behaved this way was that they had never seen a European ship before. They thought that it was the ship of their god, whom legend related, had first brought their people to these shores in a large copper canoe, and was coming to punish them for their misdeeds. The next morning the natives had recovered from the shock, and hundreds of their men and women in many canoes came out to the ship bringing furs and cedar hats to trade for metal, cloth and knives. The Spaniards had launched their longboats and were preparing to go ashore with a huge 12 foot wooden cross and take possession of the land for King Carlos III, when a sudden wind came, causing the *Santiago* to drag her anchor towards shore. Perez ordered the boats back in, and letting the anchor slip, headed out to sea. He returned to California with his huge cross, never having gone ashore.

The Spanish authorities were disappointed at Perez's failure to make a landing, and sent another expedition the next year, 1775. There were two ships this time, the *Santiago* again, this time commanded by Bruno de Hezeta, with Perez as second in command, and the schooner, *Sonora*, only 36 feet in length commanded by 31-year-old Juan Francisco de Bodega y Quadra, with 20-year-old Francisco Antonio Mourelle as mate. Quadra became the best known of all of the Spanish explorers in the north Pacific. Hezeta's instructions were to proceed to latitude 65 degrees north, which would be a little north of Nome, an impossible goal, but it shows how sketchy the information was about Alaska, especially that found in Madrid.

Hezeta went no farther north than a point somewhere on the west coast of Vancouver Island, where he made no attempt to land, but turned back, returning to Mexico. Quadra, became separated from Hezeta, perhaps not entirely by accident, and did much better. Perhaps he believed, as James Cook, the famous English explorer, is reported to have said to a young French explorer, "The man who does no more than carry out his instructions will never get very far in discovery." He pushed north, eventually reaching Alaskan waters. During August, in the vicinity of the Nass River, British Columbia, in Portland Inlet, near the present Alaskan border, they experienced unusually hot weather, due they thought to volcanic activity. They said that they saw flames from what appeared to be the mouths of a volcano. It may be that this was the eruption that natives say occurred at about this time. These lava flows can be seen today on both sides of a logging road about 50 miles north of Terrace, British Columbia.

Quadra then proceeded to Bucareli Bay, Alaska, on the west side of Prince of Wales Island, where, on August 24, 1775, perhaps in the vicinity of Cruz or Cross Island, about ten miles west of the present villages of Klawok and Craig, he took formal possession of the area for Spain. This is the same immediate area where the Russian Chirikov first sighted land in Alaska 34 years earlier on July 15, 1741. Chirikov did not set foot on land himself. The 11 armed men that he sent ashore to look for water and wood did not return. Five days later he sent two more men in another boat, and when they did not return Chirikov broke off the expedition and returned to Siberia. Evidently they had met the warlike Tlingit Indians.

When Quadra visited the Bucareli Bay area, he spent several weeks there in 1775 and again in 1779, charting the area. He had no clashes with the Tlingits, though at times as many as 80 canoes surrounded his boats and indicated that he was not welcome. Quadra made no major discoveries, found no Russian outposts, and did not reach 65 degrees north, but his charts provided the first indication of the direction of the coast north of San Francisco to 58 degrees 50 minutes north, and he sailed farther north in the Pacific Ocean than anyone but the Russians.

It was about the time of the first two Spanish explorations in 1774 and 1775, that smallpox first appeared on the west coast, even though no Europeans had landed on the coast, except for the Russians much farther north. The disease came from the interior, among the Indians of the Missouri River drainage, and swept through the tribes of the Rockies and on to the Pacific Coast. The original source is not known, whether American, French, British or Spanish. In 1792-94, Vancouver and his men saw many natives who bore the scars of this disease. This first epidemic, and those that followed, drastically reduced the numbers of the native population on the northwest Pacific Coast. At the end of his Alaskan cruise in 1775, Quadra returned to the Spanish naval base at San Blas, Mexico, located about 60 miles north of what today is Puerto Vallarta.

A shortage of available ships at San Blas did not allow any more expeditions by the Spanish until 1779, when, on February 11th, Juan de la Bodega y Quadra and Ignacio Arteaga sailed in the two frigates *Princessa* and *Favorita* with orders again to proceed to 70 degrees north. They were to search for any Russian settlements infringing on land in the Gulf of Alaska claimed by Spain, and to arrest Cook, if they could find him, for trespassing in Spanish waters. Cook was a year ahead of them, having sailed much the same route in 1778. If Quadra and Arteaga had sailed in 1778, as originally planned, they might have met, but a shortage of shipping at San Blas had delayed them. Of course they were to also make the obligatory search for the *"Northwest Passage"*, which was supposed to be a shorter route, through North America, from Europe to Asia, though the Spaniards were no longer strong believers in its existence.

The Spaniards sailed first to Bucareli Bay in Southeast Alaska, which was as far north as Quadra had gone in 1775, and spent several weeks charting and exploring. Quadra had formally taken possession of this region for Spain in 1775.

After leaving Bucareli Bay, the two Spanish ships headed north, more or less following Cook's route of the previous year, 1778, but of course were a year late in their attempts to find him. They did not encounter any Russian settlements, either, but they did chart much of the previously unexplored coast line. They raised the Cross at Port Etches on May 23, 1779, on Hinchinbroke Island, in the entrance to Prince William Sound, Alaska, and performed the ceremony taking possession in the name of the King of Spain. This place, 61 degrees north, was the northernmost latitude in which the Spaniards performed this act. Heading west from Prince William Sound, the two Spanish commanders landed at Chatham Bay at the entrance to Cook Inlet, 59 degrees 8 minutes north, and again took possession for Spain. On the 7th of August they turned south, returning to Mexico on November 25th. This expedition would have been more significant if it had not been preceded by Cook, covering much of the same waters. Neither did they find the illusive *Northwest Passage*, nor any Russian ships or settlements. Nevertheless this Spanish expedition accomplished a lot, it extended Spain's territorial claims much farther north, though Cook and the Russians had also made similar claims previously, and much charting of the previously uncharted coast was accomplished.

The Spanish government made no further explorations in the north Pacific until 1788, when they were aroused by the reports of the Frenchman, La Perouse (about whom more later), and others concerning the spread of Russian settlements and the activities of English and other trading vessels. On March 8, 1788, the Spanish naval vessels the *Princesa*, 26 guns, commanded by Esteben Jose' Martinez, and the *San Carlos*, 16 guns, under Lopez de Haro, set out from San Blas with orders to proceed to latitude 61 degrees north and then return south, examining the coastline down to Monterey, and to avoid all trouble with any Russians that they might encounter. They proceeded directly to Prince William Sound, Alaska, arriving on May 17, and eventually anchored in a harbor that they discovered on the north side of Montague Island. They went ashore, took possession, and then explored the region in their small boats until June 15. The natives they met were friendly, and some trading was done.

Martinez, like all good explorers, according to James Cook, ignored his orders to return south down the coast, and instead headed southwest, towards Kodiak and the Aleutians. The two vessels became separated, and Martinez proceeded to Trinity Island, southwest of Kodiak Island. He missed Kodiak Island and anchored on the east side of Trinity on June 24. Haro found Kodiak Island, and, notified by a native of a Russian settlement at Three Saints Bay, he visited it, the first contact between the two nations in the North Pacific. Relationships were cordial though the Russian in charge, Delarof, impressed on Haro that he was in Russian territory, and that their claim extended as far south as 52 degrees north latitude, and included six settlements with over 400 men, an exaggeration actually, but evidently done to impress the Spaniards. Delarof also told Haro that the Russians intended to send an expedition to Nootka on Vancouver Island and take possession of that important port. This was also an exaggeration as there is no evidence that this was ever planned.

Haro left Three Saints Bay and continued southwest, making contact with Martinez, anchored at Trinity Island. Then both vessels set out for Unalaska, anchoring off its northern point on July 21. Martinez took possession and was soon visited by Russians from the east side of the island. They proceeded to the Russian settlement and remained there until August 18, taking care of their sick and taking on water and supplies with the friendly assistance of the Russian commander, Daikov. Daikov was shocked to see two heavily armed foreign warships in his harbor. There was only one Russian ship present, and Russian ships were not armed, because they were private merchantmen, not allowed by the government to carry cannon. The Spaniards remained at Unalaska until August 18, during which time more information was exchanged. The Spaniards left Unalaska on August 18, and, since the season was far advanced, abandoned their original orders to cruise south down the coast, and set sail direct to Monterey and San Blas.

Flores, the Spanish Viceroy in Mexico, took the Russian threat to Nootka seriously, even though it probably was not a serious one, and, without waiting for orders from Madrid, he set about to send an expedition to Nootka. In February, 1789, Martinez and Haro, in the same two ships they had commanded the previous year, the *Princesa* and the *San Carlos*, set out to sail to Nootka, to occupy it and build a permanent establishment, hoping thereby to strengthen Spain's claim to the territory. Arriving off Nootka on May 3 Martinez was surprised to meet the *Lady Washington*, an American ship under Captain Robert Gray, the discoverer of the Columbia River. Martinez fired a shot across the *Washington's* bow, and ordered her to heave to. Gray convinced Martinez that his ships, the *Washington* and the *Columbia*, which was still at anchor in Nootka, were not involved in the fur trade and had merely been in Nootka to pick up wood and water. Satisfied, Martinez let them depart. This was actually the second year that Gray had been at Nootka, as his two ships had attempted to acquire furs from the natives. However, the ships under the command of the British captain, Meares, had monopolized the trade, making it difficult for Gray.

When Martinez entered Friendly Cove at Nootka, he not only found the *Columbia*, but the *Iphigenia* also, the latter owned by Meares, but was sailing under the Portuguese flag, and under a Captain Douglas. Martinez was a very headstrong man, and when Haro arrived on the *San Carlos* a few days later, strengthening his hand, he arrested Douglas and replaced the Portuguese flag with the Spanish, taking over the ship. A few weeks later, Martinez changed his mind, and restored the ship to Douglas, minus most of her trade goods. After purchasing supplies from the Spaniards to replace those previously taken, Douglas was allowed to depart.

The next English ship to arrive was not so lucky. It was the small *North West America* which Meares had built at Nootka the previous year, the first European ship built in the northwest. She had wintered in Hawaii with the *Iphigenia*, and on their return to Nootka, had taken off on a trading mission to the north. Martinez immediately seized the small ship and its furs, and renaming her the *Santa Gertrudis la Magna*, sent her out to explore the entrance to the Strait of Juan de Fuca.

In the meantime, Martinez completed two forts commanding the entrance to Nootka Sound and the anchorage at Friendly Cove. Earlier in the year, Meares had sent two more ships from Canton, China to Nootka, the *Princess Royal* under Captain Thomas Hudson and the *Argonaut* under Captain Colnett. The *Princess Royal* arrived at Nootka first, and had no trouble with Martinez, indeed Hudson was a witness at the ceremony when Martinez took possession of Nootka for Carlos III on June 24, 1789. When she departed Nootka, Hudson said that he was returning to the Orient, but in reality she sailed up the northwest coast to trade for furs.

When Colnett arrived later on the *Argonaut*, he experienced much different treatment by Martinez, primarily because he also had a headstrong, combative nature, similar in temperament to the Spaniard. Meares had instructed Colnett to build a fortified permanent trading post on the land that he had purchased from the Indian chief, Maquinna, the previous year. Colnett refused to recognize the Spanish claim to the region, and when he got into a heated argument with Martinez, the latter placed him under arrest, and lowering the British flag and running up that of Spain, he took possession of the ship. There was little that Colnett could do about it, because he was anchored under the guns of the new Spanish fort.

When Captain Hudson returned on *Princess Royal* on July 12, he received a much different treatment than on his previous visit. His ship was confiscated and he and his crew made prisoners aboard her. The two English ships were taken to San Blas, Mexico, and the captains and crews imprisoned there.

It was not long before fall, when a strange event took place at Nootka. A Spanish ship arrived with orders from the Viceroy of Mexico to Martinez to abandon Nootka and return to Mexico, which he did. His impulsive actions in taking the British ships and their crews during his short stay at Nootka were to have a disastrous effect on Spanish ambitions in the North Pacific, because they created what came to be known as "*The Nootka Incident*".

Meares returned to England and, giving a very biased account of what happened at Nootka, he aroused the British government and public to the point that they mobilized the navy and were ready to declare war on Spain. For Britain there was much more at stake than the matter of three little ships, their crews, and a small piece of land thousands of miles away. It was finally a chance to end once and for all Spanish claims to exclusive rights to sail and trade in the waters of the Pacific Ocean, and sovereignty along the northwest coast of America. The government in Madrid realized that they were in no condition to challenge the mighty British Navy, so wisely suggested that the matter be settled peacefully by negotiation, but not before Parliament had voted one million pounds to prepare for war with Spain, so the Spaniards knew that the British were serious about this. The negotiations resulted in the "Nootka Convention" of October 28, 1790. This gave Britain all that she was seeking, not only restitution of property and compensation for damages, but most importantly a declaration that the British were free to sail and trade throughout the Pacific Ocean, except within ten leagues, about thirty miles, of those areas occupied by Spain. So ended Spain's claim that the Pacific was a "Spanish Lake".

Spain, however, was not through with Nootka. The newly appointed Viceroy of Mexico, the Conde de Revilla Gigedo, not expecting the Spanish capitulation in the "Nootka Incident", ordered the re-occupation of Nootka, this time on a permanent basis. Don Francisco de Eliza sailed from San Blas for Nootka with three ships in February, 1790, and proceeded to rebuild the fort which Martinez had razed upon his departure. Expecting to remain for some time he built more than Martinez had, including a church, hospital, and governor's residence. He also sent Haro and Quimper in the *Princesa Real*, Meares' old ship the *Princess Royal*, to survey and chart the Strait of Juan de Fuca, and waters to the east, hoping to extend Spain's land claims. In 1791, he sent out two more ships, the *San Carlos* under his own command and the *Santa Saturnina* under Jose Maria Narvaez to continue the explorations of Haro and Quimper. They went as far north as the northern section of Georgia Strait before returning. On their return they found that they had just missed by two days the visit at Nootka by Don Alejandro Malaspina on his return from Alaskan waters.

One of the explorations that the Spaniards made while they occupied Nootka was by Lieutenant Salvador Fidalgo in 1790, to complete what Martinez had left undone. Accompanied by both Russian and English interpreters, he sailed north from Nootka on May 4, 1790, in the *Filipino*, arrived at Prince William Sound on May 23, and explored it until June 9. He then visited Cook Inlet in July, and on August 8 arrived at the Russian settlement at Kodiak. After a short visit with Delarof, the Russian in charge, he turned east and south to explore the coast line as far as Nootka, as he was instructed to do. Unfavorable weather caused him to cut his voyage short and he returned to Monterey, and then San Blas. The storms even prevented a return visit to Nootka.

Malaspina's expedition to the north Pacific was Spain's last venture into those waters, and, by far, its most ambitious and best prepared. Malaspina was one of Spain's most brilliant naval officers. In 1778, he had completed a circumnavigation of the world. In preparing for the voyage he was given a *"carte blanche"* to select the ships, equipment and crews, including scientists that he desired. Spain evidently thought that Malaspina's voyage would be an answer to the recent voyages to the North Pacific by the famous British explorer Captain James Cook, in 1778, and Frenchman La Perouse in 1786. Two corvettes, the *Descubierta* and the *Atrevida* were specially built for the voyage, and outfitted for scientific study. Several scientists were aboard when the two ships departed from Cadiz, Spain, on July 30, 1789, under Malaspina and Jose'Bustamente y Guerra. It was to be five years and two months before the voyage was completed and the two ships returned to Cadiz in 1794. The eastern coast of South America was first explored. Cape Horn was rounded and the ships arrived at Valparaiso, Chile in February, 1790. The west coast of South America was the next region explored and the *Atrevida* arrived at Acapulco, Mexico, on February 2, 1791, sailing directly there from Panama; the *Descubierta* arrived later. They eventually sailed north from Acapulco on May 1, 1791, almost two years after leaving Cadiz.

Sailing well offshore, they finally sighted land at 56 degrees 17 minutes north latitude on June 23. Their final instructions, which came to them at Acapulco, were to make another search for the illusive *"Northwest Passage"*, so they headed for Port Mulgrave (Yakutat) for wood and water before heading north to 60 degrees, as their orders specified. They remained at Port Mulgrave, named by the British explorer George Dixon in 1787, from June 27 to July 6, 1791. Their contacts with the Tlingit natives were numerous and friendly, as the Spaniards were specifically ordered to treat the natives *"humanely"*, perhaps to counteract the history of mistreatment of the native population by them in other areas. The Spaniards were constantly on guard, and so avoided trouble.

After leaving Port Mulgrave, Malaspina and Bustamente proceeded northwest to Prince William Sound, and convinced that no *"Northwest Passage"* existed in these northern regions, turned south. Their only other stop in the North Pacific was at Nootka where they arrived on August 13, 1791, and anchored in Friendly Cove. The settlement they found was substantial, the only European settlement between San Francisco and the Russians at Prince William Sound. For almost two weeks there were three Spanish ships and over 300 Spaniards at Nootka.

THE FRENCH

In August 1785 a French expedition around the world led by Jean Francois de Galaup, Comte de La Perouse, departed Brest by order of King Louis XVI in the ships *Astrolabe* and *Boussole*, the latter commanded by De Langle. They were directed to examine the northwest coast of America as part of their voyage. This may have been France's reply to the third voyage of James Cook, or perhaps an attempt to claim some part of North America to replace that lost at Quebec, when on September 13, 1759, in a 20 minute battle on the Plains of Abraham, west of Quebec City, they lost all of New France, except parts of the Maritime Provinces, to Britain. In addition to investigating the commercial possibilities they were to look for the *Northwest Passage*, if it existed. Alaska was sighted on June 23, 1786, when Mount St. Elias appeared near latitude 60 degrees. The Frenchmen had previously rounded Cape Horn and stopped in the Hawaiian Islands on the way. Turning south, they coasted along the shore line until they found Lituya Bay near Cape Fairweather, on the second of July. They entered and named it Port des Francais. Anchoring, they spent several weeks exploring and surveying. La Perouse purchased an island in the bay from a native chief and set up an astronomical station, thereby making a claim of ownership for France. He thought it would serve as a good base for fur trading activities into which he entered, acquiring about 600 sea otter and other skins.

On July 13 an unfortunate incident occurred when three small boats that had been sent out from Lituya Bay to take soundings for a chart were caught in the outflowing current at the narrow entrance and carried into the breakers of a huge tide rip. These tide rips are a common occurrence where the tidal currents flowing out of an inlet meet incoming swells and breakers. Two of the boats were carried into the breakers before they had time to avoid the danger. The boats were destroyed and 21 men, including six of the officers from the two ships, were lost. Not a man was saved, and no bodies were ever found. The third boat, the smallest of the three, was able to avoid the danger. A monument to the lost men was erected on the previously purchased island, and the island named "L'Isle du Cenotaphe" because of its monument. After leaving Lituya Bay, La Perouse sailed south along the coasts of what are now Alaska and British Columbia, returning to Hawaii for the winter. The following year, 1787, La Perouse sailed north to Kamchatka to see what the Russians were up to. While there he sent a copy of his journal for the voyage to that point, back to France. This was fortunate, as the following year, 1788, the two French ships disappeared after leaving Australia. Their fate was not known for about 40 years, when around 1828, the wrecks were found in the Solomon Islands. La Perouse and all of his men had been massacred by the natives.

In 1791, the French were again represented on the Northwest Coast, when Captain Etienne Marchand of the *Solide* first sighted the Alaska coast near Cape Edgecumbe. He had departed Marseilles at the end of 1790, on a private voyage of trade and circumnavigation. He found the natives well supplied with European goods and difficult to trade with, so had little success and moved on. This ended France's exploration into North Pacific waters. No doubt the turmoil that came to France with the Revolution that began in 1789, drew their attention to their own affairs.

THE ENGLISH

Spain was not the only European nation interested in the news that Russia was active in the North Pacific. The British government was also aware of this and also of the equally secret activities of the Spanish. The British were still interested in the possibility that the long sought for "*Northwest Passage*" might really exist. In fact, the long standing Parliamentary reward of 5,000 pounds still stood, and, in 1776, Parliament offered a new reward of 20,000 pounds to the discoverer of the "*Northwest Passage*." For the first time, they also extended these offers to ships of the Royal Navy. In 1776, the Navy decided to investigate these matters, and chose Captain James Cook to head the expedition. Cook had previously headed two very successful expeditions to the South Pacific and Antarctic, and was Britain's most famous explorer.

Cook had two ships assigned to him, his old ship from his second cruise, the 460 ton *Resolution*, and the *Discovery*, a 300 ton collier. He also carried, as he did on his second voyage, some of the new chronometers, which, when combined with the sextant, made possible more accurate determination of the longitude of a position. In July, 1776, Cook departed England, just as the revolution in the American Colonies began. Cook rounded Africa at the Cape of Good Hope and first proceeded across the Indian Ocean to Tasmania, then New Zealand and Tahiti. On January 18, 1778, he discovered some islands that he called the Sandwich Islands, after the Earl of Sandwich, a First Lord of the Admiralty. These are known today as the Hawaiian Islands. In early February he resumed his voyage and arrived at a point off the coast of today's Oregon, where he headed north along the coastline. Bad weather kept the ships well off the coast, thus missing the Columbia River and the Strait of Juan de Fuca. On March 29, the ships were off the west coast of Vancouver Island, where they anchored in Resolution Cove in Nootka Sound, or King George's Sound, as Cook called it. Thirty or 40 canoes filled with natives came out to greet them. Cook had no idea that the Spaniard, Perez, had preceded him at Nootka in 1774. The next day the natives returned, anxious to trade skins and food for iron primarily; they had little interest in beads. Cook had little interest in acquiring furs, but many of his men, knowing that they were heading for some cold climates to the north, acquired furs to keep them warm. They had no idea of the real value of these furs, especially those of the sea otter. When Cook and his men went ashore, they were the first Europeans to set foot on British Columbia soil, as Perez, in 1774, had not done so. The Spanish explorer, Quadra, had landed at several points in Alaska in 1775.

Four weeks of hard work was performed in repairing the two ships. They both needed caulking, and one needed a new mizzenmast and repairs to its foremast. Water casks were filled, and extra spars cut for future use. A brewery was set up to brew "spruce beer", an antiscorbutic to prevent scurvy. Cook was always careful to take all possible steps to ward off this disease, which was, at that time, the scourge of all mariners.

During Cook's stay at Nootka, the relationship between the English and the Nootka natives was generally very good, though the English had difficulty adjusting to the natives propensity to thievery, especially of any pieces of metal that were handy. The only bloodshed was a small amount when Cook, exasperated when some natives took some iron and refused to return it, fired at them with a load of buckshot from a musket hitting them in their "backs and backsides".

While he was in Nootka Sound, Cook did some exploring of its various arms, and went around Bligh Island, thereby proving it to be an island. He named the island after one of his officers, William Bligh, later of "Mutiny on the Bounty" fame. On April 26, the two ships raised anchors and were towed out of Nootka Sound by the oarsmen of their small boats. They headed north, saw and named Mount Edgecumbe near Sitka, and Mount Fairweather on the mainland, near Glacier Bay, and commenced a search for a waterway as they headed northwest along the coastline. They stopped at Kayak Island to place a bottle containing the names of the two ships, the date of the discovery and two British coins. Cook then explored Prince William Sound, and later Cook Inlet, which he took to be a river. Deciding that if any waterway existed, it must be much farther north, he sailed through the Aleutian

Island Chain, across the Bering Sea, and through the Bering Strait until stopped by the icepack at 70 degrees 29 minutes latitude, only about 130 miles from Point Barrow. Returning south, he re-provisioned in the Aleutians and then proceeded south to winter in the Hawaiian Islands. On February 14, 1779, Cook was killed by the natives while ashore trying to recover a boat which had been stolen.

Captain Charles Clerke took over from Cook and continued the exploration of Bering Strait. Going up the Asian side of the strait this year, 1779, they were stopped by the ice at about the same latitude as the previous year, 70 degrees. They turned south and explored the Siberian coastline, returning to Petropavlovsk. Captain Clerke, who was very ill when they left the Hawaiian Islands, died a few days before they reached the Russian port. Lieutenant Gore, next in rank, took over command of the *Resolution*, and Lieutenant King the *Discovery*. Leaving Petropavlovsk after repairing the ships, which had been damaged by the ice, they proceeded south to the Chinese port of Canton. Events that occurred there were to have a tremendous impact on the North Pacific Coast of North America. A brisk trade sprang up between Chinese merchants and the crew members for the sea otter skins that they had purchased to keep warm. The furs brought such extremely high prices that the crews wanted to return immediately to North America, get some more furs and make their fortunes. Gore had difficulty avoiding a mutiny. The ships had an uneventful voyage home, reaching England in October, 1780. The American Revolution had spread to a world wide conflict against France and Spain, and Cook's ships and their crews went to war. For the time being, voyages of exploration were forgotten.

The official account of Cook's voyage was not published until June, 1784, because of the large amount of material it covered. It sold out in just three days, made public the account of the Chinese demand for sea otter furs, and the rush to the Pacific Northwest was on. The first non-Russian fur trader was the British Captain Hanna, who left China on April 15, 1785, and arrived off Nootka on August 9. He traded successfully, though not peacefully with the natives, and, after five weeks, left on a return voyage to China. The cargo of 560 sea otter skins sold for 20,600 Spanish dollars.

Leaving discussion of the development of the fur trade to the next chapter, let us turn our attention to the Englishman who had a greater impact on the coast of Northwestern North America, especially the waters between Olympia, Washington, and Skagway, Alaska, that we now call "The Inside Passage", than any other person. This man was Captain George Vancouver of the Royal Navy. He was born at King's Lynn, Norfolk, a North Sea port about 100 miles north of London on June 22, 1757. He joined the Royal Navy at the age of fourteen and sailed on the *Resolution* under Cook when he left England on July,

1772, on his second voyage, when he made a polar circumnavigation of the Antarctic and cruised the South Seas during the Antarctic winters. He was also with Cook on his third voyage when he explored the North Pacific, and was eventually killed in Hawaii. In fact, Vancouver was in the shore party with Cook when the latter was slain by the Hawaiian natives.

Vancouver was 23 years of age when he returned to England from the third voyage and, two weeks later, he passed his examinations and was commissioned a lieutenant, his first commission. During the years from 1781-89, Vancouver served aboard warships that made two cruises to the Caribbean Sea. During that period he was at times engaged in surveying and charting various harbors, including large Kingston Harbor in Jamaica, which experience undoubtedly affected his future career, as he became a proficient cartographer.

After agreement on the Nootka Sound Convention at Madrid in November, 1790, England made plans to take over the property seized by the Spaniard, Martinez, at Nootka in 1789. Vancouver was named to command this expedition, and in addition to visiting Nootka, was also ordered to make an accurate survey of the Pacific coastline from 30 degrees north latitude to Cook's Inlet. While surveying and charting all of these waters, Vancouver was also to make one more search for "The Northwest Passage." Vancouver was given two ships to carry out this expedition. The *Discovery*, which he would command, was a threemasted full-rigged ship, with a total complement of 101 persons. The *Chatham*, a two-masted brig of 130 tons was selected as the consort, or escort vessel, under the command of Lieutenant William Broughton. The officers of the *Discovery* were personally selected by Vancouver, two of the three lieutenants, Peter Puget and Joseph Baker and the master Joseph Whidbey, had been shipmates of his in cruises to the Caribbean. The First Lieutenant was Zachary Mudge. Before joining the *Discovery*, Vancouver spent a month at the Admiralty offices during which the objectives of the voyage were presented, and he had the opportunity to voice his own opinions.

On April 1, 1791, the two ships departed Falmouth on what was to be one of the longest continuous voyages in history. Having his choice of routes to the Pacific, Vancouver followed Cook's example and chose the Cape of Good Hope route. After re-provisioning at Capetown, at the southern tip of Africa, the Cape of Good Hope, the last opportunity for many months, Vancouver sailed to Australia, where he explored and surveyed the south and southwest coasts. Prior to this, these areas were nearly blank on the maps. He next sailed to Dusky Bay, New Zealand, where the ships spent three weeks. The next stop was at Tahiti for a month of repairing and re-provisioning the ships, and making astronomical observations.

In January, 1792, Vancouver left Tahiti, bound for the Hawaiian

Islands, where he expected to meet a storeship as specified in his instructions. Landfall was made on the island of Hawaii on March 1. After visiting the islands of Hawaii, Oahu, Kauai and Niihau, the ships departed for North America, without meeting the expected store ship. On April 18, 1792, just over a year since leaving England, the coast of New Albion, (the British still used the name that Drake had given to that part of the world), was sighted near Cape Mendocino about 110 miles north of San Francisco Bay. Here began the remarkable hydrographic survey, unique in scope, accuracy and thoroughness, that was Vancouver's greatest accomplishment. His instructions were to examine and survey the coast between latitudes 30 degrees north and 60 degrees north latitude, an airline distance of about 1800 miles, but many times more when the numerous long inlets and islands are included. It took him three summer seasons of hard, intensive work to accomplish this task. The only descriptions of that intricate coast that Vancouver had to work with were the general chart made on Cook's third voyage, and some charts made by British traders on small sections of the coast. The Spaniards had done considerable surveying, but since they did not publish their charts, in order to maintain secrecy about their efforts, the northwest coast was basically uncharted territory.

In order to either find or make sure that the "Northwest Passage" did not exist, Vancouver's method, after making a landfall that was certain on the mainland, was to follow that shoreline all of the way north to 60 degrees, Prince William Sound, Alaska. From Cape Mendocino north to the Strait of Juan de Fuca the coast line is relatively straight and with few good harbors. Surveying in this section was done from the large ships, by taking numerous different bearings on prominent landmarks as they sailed along a straight, carefully measured course two to five miles offshore. All of this information was recorded and, together with depth soundings, was later used in preparing the charts and numerous drawings to accompany them. When darkness fell, the ships moved offshore and returned the next morning to pick up the survey at the point where they had quit the previous evening.

Stormy weather and frequent poor visibility conditions, made the task more difficult, resulting in delays. This type of surveying was continued all of the way up to the Strait of Juan de Fuca, where the coastline takes on a completely different aspect. On April 25, Vancouver rounded Cape Flattery, which was noted and named by Cook, and entered the Strait, anchoring a few miles east.

In ten days the two ships had surveyed about 350 miles of the coastline, but that was the easy part, from here on it would be more tedious and much slower. They had made, however, what some people regarded as a big error in that they had not discovered the Columbia River, as they passed that section of the coast. They recognized from the mud and debris that they encountered in the water that a major river was near, but because of poor visibility, were unable to locate it. Rather than waste time, Vancouver decided to push on, and to examine the river when he returned. He was much chagrined when, two days later, he met the man who is given credit for discovering the Columbia, Captain Robert Gray in the American fur trading ship *Columbia*, out of Boston. This was the first ship the expedition had seen since leaving the Cape of Good Hope, eight months earlier. Captain Gray had entered the river and named it Columbia, after his ship. In addition to informing Vancouver of his discovery of the Columbia River, Gray also told him that he had sailed into the Strait of Juan de Fuca, which was just a short distance farther north from where they were, but he had gone in only for about 50 miles or so. On the return voyage that fall, Broughton took the *Chatham* into the Columbia River and took his small boats about 100 miles up river, as far as Portland, Oregon today, much farther than Gray had gone. After entering the Strait of Juan de Fuca, the ships sailed east keeping to the mainland shore. On May 1, Vancouver found what he was looking for, a good, secure harbor which he named Port Discovery, where the *Discovery* and *Chatham* could remain while the small boats were sent out to continue the survey. This method of surveying by the small boats, under sail when the wind obliged, and propelled by oars by the crew most of the time, was used from this point on for the next three years, as the expedition headed north. In these restricted waters, with strong currents in many places, it was the only possible method.

Vancouver thought that he had now penetrated the Strait farther than Captain Gray had, and that he was the first European to enter these waters. He had no way of knowing that the Spaniards had been there before him. In 1790, Manuel Quimper along with Haro, in the *Princesa Real*, Meares old ship the *Princess Royal*, had anchored in Port Discovery, and on July 13, 1790, had taken possession of the territory in the name of Carlos III of Spain. He had named the area "Quadra" after that Spanish explorer, now commandant at San Blas. Quimper at Port Discovery was at the entrance to Puget Sound, but thought that it was only a bay, so did not investigate it. On the way out of the Strait, Quimper stopped at Neah Bay on July 24, 1790, and on August 1, 1790 took possession for Spain. The following year, 1791, Don Francisco de Eliza, at that time commander at Nootka, had entered the Strait in the *San Carlos*, along with Jose Maria Narvaez in the *Santa Saturnina*. They intended to complete the investigations made the previous year by Quimper. They sailed north and entered what is now called Georgia Strait and sailed almost to the northern end, past Texada Island.

Before starting north on his survey, Vancouver first had to investigate those waters that opened to the south. This was done by the crews and officers in the small boats. The complete survey of this inland sea, including all of its various arms, was completed in the month of May. A two boat expedition under Lieutentant Puget and Master Joseph Whidbey traced the whole upper part of Puget Sound in eight days working from day break to dusk. For his efforts, Vancouver named these waters Puget Sound. This name has since been extended to include the waters to those north of Seattle, all of the way up to the southern tip of Whidbey Island, named after Joseph Whidbey, master of the *Discovery*. Vancouver himself led two boats into what is now known as Commencement Bay, the site of modern Tacoma, and named Mount Rainier, which dominates the landscape, for his friend from the Caribbean cruises, Captain Peter Rainier.

During these explorations, Vancouver and his men, especially the biologist Menzies, were taken with the beauty and general character of the region, describing it as one of the most beautiful they had seen, and projecting a great future for its settlement. Anyone who has visited western Washington in the springtime can appreciate why they were so impressed.

Having completed the survey of Puget Sound, the two ships headed north, still following the mainland shore. On June 22, 1792, near the site of present day Vancouver, British Columbia, Captain Vancouver discovered the two Spanish survey vessels, *Sutil* and *Mexicana*. Visiting them, he was apprised of their mission, and was astounded to see how small the ships were, and how poorly equipped they were, in his opinion, for the work assigned to them. Broughton, in the *Chatham*, had encountered the two small Spanish ships earlier, on June 13, near the present day United States/Canada border.

The Spaniards reported that Quadra was already at Nootka, awaiting Vancouver's arrival, but since the latter had not met his store ship carrying his orders for the negotiations, and since he was also anxious to get as much of the survey completed as possible this first summer, he ignored this news. Vancouver's orders were to assist any Spanish vessels that he met, so in spite of finding them to have preceded him, he suggested that they exchange information and continue their surveys jointly. The Spaniards readily agreed, and the four ships, and their small boats continued the survey north and west, investigating each of the many inlets they encountered. These joint efforts continued for about three weeks and the relationship between the British and Spanish officers and crews was very cordial.   Vancouver had sent Johnstone to the northwest through the islands north of the Strait of Georgia to find a possible way through. When Johnstone returned, saying that he had found a passage and had continued until he could see the open ocean, it was clear that the land mass to the west was an island, called Vancouver Island today, and that the ships could proceed that way. Vancouver decided to do that, and continue the survey from a point farther north, avoiding the numerous "*rapids*" that lay ahead. The Spaniards insisted that their orders were to stick to the mainland shore, so the two groups parted amicably, agreeing to meet later in the summer at Nootka.

On July 14, Vancouver took his two ships through Discovery Passage, past today's settlement of Campbell River on Vancouver Island, through the turbulent waters of Seymour Narrows, and northwest through Johnstone Strait, named for the man who discovered it, to the more open waters of Queen Charlotte Strait. Vancouver had chosen the only navigable route through the Discovery Islands as they are known today, the one used ever since by ships traversing the Inside Passage.

After passing through Johnstone Strait, Vancouver took the two ships to the mainland, where they went back and picked up the survey where they had previously quit, and brought it forward. This was a slow tedious task due to the number and size of the inlets. For example 70 mile long Knight Inlet, one of the longest on the coast, was only one of the many surveyed.

On Monday, August 4 the *Chatham* had finished the survey of this area, and they worked their way down Fife Sound to the more open waters of Queen Charlotte Strait, where they could continue northwest. On August 6, 1792, the expedition almost came to an end when the *Discovery* grounded hard, with no warning, at high tide on a rocky ledge that Vancouver named Mary Rock, as it is still shown on today's charts, about 15 miles north of present day Port Hardy, British Columbia. Because the tide was falling rapidly, it was necessary to off-load as much of their supplies as possible into the small boats, and to dump their water, wood and even some of the ballast. To keep the *Discovery* from capsizing as the water dropped, she was propped up with spars and spare masts. Fortunately the seas were calm, and there were no swells from the nearby Pacific. They came very close to losing the *Discovery*, but she was pulled off the rocks when high tide righted her at about 2:00 a.m. By noon everything had been brought back aboard and restowed. They were ready to proceed. They didn't go far, however, as at 6:00 p.m. on August 7, the *Chatham* grounded on another rock, and was in real danger, but came off on high tide at 1:30 a.m. on the 8th. Fortunately neither ship suffered any serious damage. Vancouver, like all of the other sailors in these previously uncharted waters located rocks the hard way; he hit them.

Following these two groundings, the most serious of the entire four year voyage, the ships continued north across Queen Charlotte Sound, and past Cape Caution, which Vancouver named the following year, 1793, when he returned to continue the survey. The name resulted from the groundings of the two ships in 1792. After crossing Queen Charlotte Sound the ships reached Calvert Island and passed into Fitzhugh Sound, between Calvert Island and the mainland. They were heading for Port Safety, now Safety Cove, on Calvert Island, which had been described to Vancouver by an English trader, Captain Duncan.

Finding a good anchorage, fresh water and a source of wood, the two ships anchored on August 10, 1792, and soon sent the small boats out surveying. Puget and Whidbey went south to trace the shoreline they had passed on their way to Port Safety, and Vancouver, Johnstone and Mr. Humphreys, a master's mate from the *Chatham*, set out to the north. Vancouver returned after four days, leaving the other two boats to continue the work.

While Vancouver was waiting for the return of the boats, an English trading vessel, the *Venus*, came in and anchored. Her captain reported that the long awaited storeship, *Daedalus*, was at Nootka waiting for Vancouver, and that Quadra was also waiting, impatiently, for his arrival so that he could turn over the disputed land to Vancouver. The sad news was that the captain of the *Daedalus*, Lieutenant Hergest and Mr. Gooch, an astronomer being sent to Vancouver, had both been killed by natives in the Hawaiian Islands. Hergest had been Vancouver's closest friend for many years, and had also been on Cook's voyages.

The news caused Vancouver to discontinue the survey for the year as soon as the boats returned. On the 19th of August the *Discovery* and *Chatham* sailed for Nootka, on the west coast of Vancouver Island, where they anchored on August 28. Vancouver sent Puget ashore to announce his arrival and to tell Quadra that he would salute the Spanish flag if Quadra would return the salute to the English flag. Quadra agreed, and 13 gun salutes from each side opened the formalities at Nootka. Quadra and Vancouver had been selected by their respective countries to negotiate the transfer of land and property at Nootka that had been taken from the British in 1789. This was in accord with the Nootka Sound Convention between Spain and Britain. The two men were soon on very good terms, in fact, they became fast friends, due partly to Quadra's hospitality. Quadra provided all ships that came into Nootka, both warships and commercial traders, a daily supply of hot rolls, fresh milk, and vegetables from the gardens. He understood the hardships of shipboard life well, since he had taken a 36 foot vessel from San Blas, Mexico, to Prince William Sound in Alaska in 1775.

Despite their friendship, Quadra and Vancouver could not agree on just what was supposed to be transferred by Spain to England, primarily because their orders conflicted. The orders did state that if they could not agree, the problem would be referred back to their respective governments. This is what occurred. The inability to come to an agreement did not affect the relationship between Quadra and Vancouver, in fact, on his charts Vancouver named the big island on which Nootka is situated "Quadra y Vancouver," or "Quadra and Vancouver". However, the British Admiralty thought this name too long, and dropped Quadra's name. His name was later given to the much smaller Quadra Island, across Discovery Passage from Vancouver Island.

Vancouver stayed at Nootka for six weeks, departing for California in mid-October. The two small Spanish survey ships, the *Mexicana* and the *Sutil*, that had joined Vancouver earlier in the year in Georgia Strait, arrived at Nootka shortly after he did, having completed their survey work, making a circumnavigation of Vancouver Island.

After leaving Nootka, the three British ships sailed for California, stopping at San Francisco and Monterey before heading for the Hawaiian Islands, where they spent the winter.

Sailing from the Hawaiian Islands at the end of March, 1793, the *Discovery* and *Chatham* sailed to the Northwest Coast to resume the surveys at the points where they ceased the previous year, near Bella Coola, British Columbia.

During this part of their work, they missed meeting Alexander Mackenzie by only a few weeks. MacKenzie was an explorer for the Northwest Fur Company of Montreal, and had made the first crossing of the North American continent north of Mexico. His was a tremendous feat of exploration, preceding Lewis and Clark's journey by twelve years. When he was threatened by Bella Bella natives in Dean Channel he turned back, but not before painting on a rock face, "Alexander Mackenzie, by land from Canada, July 22, 1793." He then retraced his route to the fur trading post on the Peace River where they had begun their journey that spring. The party was small, Mackenzie and another Scot, six French Canadian "voyageurs", and two Indian hunters, in a 25 foot canoe. They had cached the canoe and supplies on the Fraser River when it became impassable, and had walked the last 300 miles, through and over the mountains to Bella Coola, and then by Indian dugouts to Dean Channel, where they were forced to turn around.

Keeping to the mainland shore, Vancouver, with the two ships and their boats, continued their surveys into what is now Alaska, to a point near present day Petersburg, Alaska. Near the end of September, 1794, the survey was discontinued for that year, as the weather was getting stormy. On their return to the Hawaiian Islands, Vancouver made more surveys on the Queen Charlotte Islands, and in California.

In the middle of March, 1794, Vancouver and his two ships departed the Hawaiian Islands for the last time. They headed straight for Cook Inlet in Alaska. While surveying Cook Inlet, the British met some parties of Russian fur traders, and found them to be well established in that activity. Vancouver just missed meeting the Russian manager, Baranof, but after waiting for several days for his expected arrival, he left to continue surveying. From Cook Inlet the British ships moved to Prince William Sound where nearly a month was spent surveying. In June the Chatham departed to examine the coastline from Prince William Sound to Yakutat Bay. The Discovery followed in a few days. It was Vancouver's plan to continue the survey south to the point where it was discontinued the previous year, at Cape Decision.

The ships continued down the coastline to Cape Spencer, where following the coastline they turned into Cross Sound. The two ships found a suitable anchorage in Port Althorp, near present day Elfin Cove, and the survey continued in the small boats. They sailed by present day Glacier Bay National Park, seeing only a wall of ice. In 1794, Glacier Bay did not exist, it was filled by a glacier, several hundred feet thick. Cross Sound was difficult to navigate as it was partly filled with floating ice from the glaciers.

Whidbey started his boat surveys at Cape Spencer, at the entrance to Cross Sound and traced the mainland shore through Icy Strait and into Lynn Canal, which Vancouver named for his birthplace in England. The northern end of Lynn Canal, now Skagway, Alaska, is the northern end of the Inside Passage. He then proceeded down Chatham Strait along the west side of Admiralty Island, thinking that it was part of the mainland, until he could see at a distance Cape Decision, where the previous year's survey had been discontinued. Whidbey later realized his error in not recognizing Admiralty as an island, and returned to the mainland to continue the survey.

Vancouver's final anchorage in the Northwest was at Port Conclusion on the south end of Baranof Island. From there two boat crews under Whidbey and Johnstone were sent out to complete the survey. The two crews met near Point Vandeput, about ten miles north of present day Petersburg, Alaska, completing the first survey of the North Pacific coast, from Monterey, California to Cook Inlet, Alaska. It was also the first survey of the Inside Passage from Olympia, Washington, to Skagway, Alaska. The voyage settled once and for all the nonexistence of a "Northwest Passage". Returning to the ships at Port Conclusion, there was a big celebration of a job well done. A southeast gale with heavy rain delayed the departure for four days, and on August 22, 1794, they began their return cruise. Stopping at Nootka one last time, they prepared the well worn ships for the long voyage. After waiting a month for further orders and mail, they finally gave up and set out for home on October 16, 1794. The Discovery arrived at Deal, England, on the 15th of October, 1795, and the Chatham at Plymouth the following day. This was one of the longest voyages on record, taking four years and six and a half months, and, about 65,000 miles for the Discovery and Chatham plus another 10,000 miles for the small boats on their surveys.

Vancouver was always concerned about the health and welfare

of his men, especially in the avoidance of scurvy. The *Discovery* lost six men during the voyage, one from disease, one from poison, eating bad shellfish, one suicide and three through accidents. These losses were about one-third the normal death rate in England at that time. The *Chatham* did not lose a man on the entire voyage.

Vancouver's own health had been declining in the last year of the voyage, preventing him from making some of the small boat surveys himself. He died at Petersham, England, on May 12, 1798, at the age of 40. He had completed work on five of the six volumes of the account of his voyage, and was halfway through the sixth when he died. His brother, John, with the help of Peter Puget, completed the last volume.

BARANOF

At the time that Captain George Vancouver was departing from England on his momentous voyage to the North Pacific, another man, who was also destined to play a most important role in the history of that area, was arriving on the scene. He was Alexander Baranof, who had been employed by Gregory Shelekhov, the founder of the settlement of Three Saints Bay on Kodiak Island in 1784, to be the new manager of his affairs at Kodiak. Baranof had departed from Okhotsk, Siberia, on August 10, 1790, in the ship *The Three Saints*, planning to go directly to Kodiak. On September 28, the ship put into the port of Unalaska in the Aleutians for water, since her water casks all leaked and they had run out of that precious commodity. A storm came up while *The Three Saints* was at anchor and it blew the ship onto the rocky shore. All the crew and passengers were safe, and they were able to save some of the cargo, but they were stranded at Unalaska for the fast approaching winter.

Baranof was 43 years old at the time, and had been a successful fur trader at Ivhutsk in Siberia until the natives robbed him of his furs, and he was broke. He was in a receptive mood when Shelekhov approached him with the opportunity to go to Russian America as his representative.

Baranof did not waste his time while marooned at Unalaska, he learned as much as he could about the people with whom he would have to deal, the native Aleuts, and the Russian *promyshlenniki*. He also had three large sea lion skin boats built to take the party to Kodiak. Toward the end of April they set out from Unalaska, and on the 27th of June, 1791, they arrived at Three Saints Bay, Kodiak. Baranof, very sick and delirious with fever, had to be carried ashore, an inauspicious arrival.

Baranof soon recovered, and took over command of all of Shelekhov's establishments. He imposed very strict discipline on the Russians. The village was full of half-Russian children, and Baranof regulated relations between the Russians and the Aleut women, a frequent source of trouble. A man had to stay with the woman that he chose, with her consent and with that of her parents. She in effect became his wife. Baranof got along well with the natives, he had to, as they were his source of manpower. He learned their language, and listened to their problems. He used the Aleuts as hunters in their two-man biadarkas (kayaks), to take the sea otters as his predecessors had done. Baranof also had to deal with the competition from several other Russian companies that had settlements and traders in Russian America. They were a constant source of trouble. There was also the competition to the south and east from the ships of the English and American fur traders. These latter traders had advantages over the Russians. They had built no forts or trading posts that were expensive to maintain, they had much better ships, and their lines of communication to their home bases were less costly and safer than those of the Russians, who had to transport everything across Siberia before they could load it into their ships.

In 1792, Shelekhov sent a supply ship, the *Eagle*, with some supplies and an Englishman, Shields, who was knowledgeable in shipbuilding. Baranof was told, with the help of Shields and some men sent with him, to construct a shipyard, and build two ships. Though this seemed like an impossible task with the meager supplies that were sent, Baranof obeyed the orders. Since the trees on Kodiak Island were not large enough, Baranof sent Shields and his men to Resurrection Bay, on the east side of the Kenai Peninsula, near present day Seward, to set up his shipyard. In August of 1794, the first ship was launched, and named the *Phoenix*. It was 73 feet long with a beam of 23 feet. She was placed in service for trips from Russian America to Okhotsk, and performed this service for several years until she was lost in a storm in the Gulf of Alaska. On her maiden voyage, the trip to Asia was accomplished in about a month, an unprecedented speed for a Russian ship on that run.

This first success was followed by the construction of two smaller ships, the 45 foot *Dolphin* and the 35 foot *Olga* in 1795. With these ships Baranof was able to send an armed escort vessel along with the Aleut hunters in their biadarkas on the sea otter hunting trips. When they had been sent out along the mainland coast without this protection they were harassed and killed by the warlike Tlingits, who had troubled the Russians ever since Chirikov lost two boat crews to them when he had made a futile attempt to get water and wood on the west coast of Prince of Wales Island.

For several years it was Baranof's intention to go to Sitka and establish a post there to counter the inroads of the British and American traders who came there each year to trade for the sea otter furs.

In April of 1799, Baranof set out from Kodiak in two of his locally built ships, the *Olga* and the *Konstantin* and a fleet of nearly 200 two-man biadarkas. Passing by Prince William Sound, they were joined by Baranof's most trusted assistant, Kushof, and an additional 150 biadarkas. Misfortune met the expedition, first in the form of a storm, which took 30 of the biadarkas and their two-man crews, and then a night raid by the Tlingits on their camp. Another 13 biadarkas and their men were lost.

Baranof, nevertheless, pressed on and arrived at a point known as Old Sitka. A crowd of Tlingit natives gathered, they had a large village about six miles south, near the present town of Sitka. From one of their chiefs, Baranof purchased, with beads and other trade goods, a site on which to locate the buildings that he intended to erect. The next day Baranof was visited by a Boston ship, the *Caroline* under Captain Cleveland. The American warned the Russians of the war-like Tlingits who had tried to capture his ship as he traded with them for sea otter furs. A fort was erected and named St. Michael. Several other American ships visited during the summer as the construction was proceeding.

The Tlingits were a real menace to the Russians, because they were not only warlike, but they were well provided with firearms, ammunition and alcohol from the British and American traders. Recognizing the dangers of arming the natives, the Russians, and the Spaniards also farther south, always refused to trade for these items, though they were much in demand by the natives,

Thinking that the settlement at Sitka was secure, Baranof returned to his base at Kodiak in 1801, leaving 300 colonists, Russian and Aleut at Sitka. Good news awaited him at Kodiak, first the Tsar Alexander I had approved the creation, on August 11, 1799, of the Russian American Company which was to have a monopoly in the American fur trade for 25 years, removing all of Baranof's Russian competition. Secondly, Baranof was named as resident manager and Governor of Russian America, now Alaska, and was raised to the rank of "Collegiate Councilor", entitled to be called Excellency. This latter rank would make him a social equal of the naval officers, who had always been a thorn in his side, refusing to deal with him since he was a mere merchant. All of this would make Baranof's job easier

Peace was short-lived, however, because in June, 1802 the Tlingits attacked at Sitka while most of the men were off hunting, and captured and burned the fort and other buildings. Three Russian men, 18 Aleut women and a few Aleut hunters escaped and were picked up by a British ship, whose Captain Barber took them to Kodiak, and returned them to Baranof. Barber exacted a 10,000 ruble, about $5,000, ransom, which naturally outraged the Russian. Baranof had no choice but to comply.

In the spring of 1804, Baranof set out to retake Sitka from the Tlingits. He had 120 Russians in four of his small ships and 400 biadarkas with their two man crews. When Baranof's flotilla arrived at Sitka, he was overjoyed to see the 450 ton Russian frigate, *Neva*, under the command of Captain Lisiansky, anchored in the harbor waiting to assist him in the forthcoming battle. The arrival of the *Neva*, was very fortuitous, as it was her guns that settled the outcome of the two day battle. After considerable losses on both sides, the Tlingits abandoned their fortified position, and the Russians burned it to the ground. The site of the Battle of Sitka is now the Sitka National Historical Park, in commemoration of this battle, the last between the Russians and the Tlingits in the Sitka area. Baranof began building a new fort near the battleground, and named it New Archangel, but it was always known as Sitka. Baranof moved his headquarters to Sitka from Kodiak after the construction at the former place was completed. Thus ended his worst struggles in his years as manager of the Russian America Company and as Governor of Russian America.

More and more American and English trading ships came into Sitka each year and Baranof expanded his sea otter hunting territory all of the way to the California coast. In 1812, the Russians purchased land in California, 75 miles north of San Francisco, opened a trading post, and established an agricultural colony in the hope of providing food for the settlements in Russian America. The colony operated for 30 years, but always at a loss. It was finally sold in 1841 for $30,000 to an American, John Sutter, who became famous when gold was discovered at his mill near Sacramento in 1848, setting off the big California Gold Rush of 1849.

Baranof was finally relieved of his duties in 1818 after serving in Alaska for 27 years. He died at Batavia, Dutch East Indies, on April 16, 1819, on his way home to Russia. He was 72 years old.

Thirteen governors followed Baranof at Sitka, which for many years, remained the most important port in the Pacific. It became American territory on October 18, 1867, with the purchase orchestrated by Secretary Seward for $7,200,000.

AMERICANS

The only American ships in North Pacific waters in the eighteenth century were those of private fur traders. The young American

Government, trying to survive and get established after the Revolution, did not have the time or resources to do any exploring that far from their capital of Philadelphia. The first trader on the scene was Captain Robert Gray in his ship, the *Lady Washington*, and with him Kendrick in the *Columbia*. They arrived at Nootka in 1788. They returned for several years, and in 1792 Gray discovered the Columbia River, and named it for the ship he was commanding that year, the *Columbia*. Many other American ships traded along the coastlines of what are now British Columbia and Alaska, but they were primarily after furs, and exploration was definitely a secondary interest. The only official United States Government sponsored expedition to the Pacific Northwest was overland by Lewis and Clark from St. Louis to the mouth of the Columbia River in 1804-6.

The Bastion, built in 1853 by the Hudson's Bay Company, is now a museum located on the hillside above Nanaimo Harbour.

CHAPTER FOUR

FUR TRADERS

The Northwest Coast of North America and the waters of the North Pacific Ocean have five principal resources that first attracted Europeans. They were (1) fur bearing mammals, (2) minerals, (3) fish and shellfish, (4) timber, and (5) whales. It is logical to begin with the fur bearing mammals, specifically, the sea otter, because they are the resource that first brought outsiders to this area.

The natives, of course, took the sea otter for their furs long before the arrival of the white men. They used the furs for garments, and also traded them to tribes in the interior where they were not available. Sea otter fur is said to be superior to any other fur. The Chinese certainly thought so, they were the first big market for them. The fur was valued because of its softness, beauty, thickness and density. The reason that the sea otter developed such fur is that unlike other sea mammals, such as the fur seals and sea lions, the otter does not have a thick layer of fat, or blubber to protect it from the very cold waters in which it lives, only its thick fur.

To preserve the insulating quality of the fur, and to insure that the air that is trapped in the fur stays in place, the fur must be kept absolutely clean to prevent water from reaching the skin. Soiled fur allows water to penetrate, causing the animal to chill and die. Much of a sea otter's time is spent grooming and cleaning its fur. For this reason, oil spills, such as the one in Prince William Sound, present a special hazard to the sea otter.

The sea otter spends most of its life afloat in the salt water, rarely coming ashore. It sleeps afloat, tied into floating strands of kelp, and eats while floating on its back. It is one of the few animals to make use of tools. It uses a rock, which it places on its chest to crack open shells of shellfish by banging them against the rock. It also takes a rock along on its dives to hammer abalone loose from the rocks to which they have attached themselves. The sea otter also has a beneficial environmental effect when they eat the sea urchins that feed on the kelp beds. This is one of their favorite meals. They have almost eliminated the urchins in some areas. These kelp beds are a very important element in the food chain, because they provide shelter for the small fish on which other fish feed.

At the beginning of the eighteenth century it is estimated that at least 150,000 sea otters lived on the west coast of North America, from Alaska to California. Over hunting decimated the sea otter herds, and by 1911, when the animals were finally protected in Alaska, by United States law, their number had been reduced to between 1,000 and 2,000, mostly in Alaskan waters. By 1929 they were extinct in British Columbia waters. The sea otter has responded positively to the ban on hunting, and it is now estimated that the numbers in Alaska are almost back to the levels of pre-European exploitation. A restocking operation on the west coast of Vancouver Island in 1972 was successful. From an original group of 46 they have grown to over 400.

During the 1920's there were several attempts to raise Arctic Blue Fox in fur farms on various islands in Southeast Alaska, along the Inside Passage. The availability of plentiful cheap food in the form of salmon, was a factor in locating these fur farms. Eventually, for one reason or another, the farms were unsuccessful and disappeared.

When the Hudson's Bay Company established forts and traded, from Taku, Alaska to the Columbia River, the furs of land mammals were brought from the interior to the coast for shipment back to the company's headquarters in London. Beaver was the most important of these furs, but mink, marten, river otter, the smaller relative of the sea otter, and bear were also taken.

The Russians, as noted in previous chapters, were the first traders drawn to the North Pacific, seeking the furs of the sea otter, fox and fur seal. At first the method of collecting the furs was to take a boat full of promyshlenniki, Russian trappers, beach the boat on one of the Aleutian Islands, and spend the winter. Male Aleuts were forced, or in some instances paid, to hunt for the Russians, who departed at the end of the next summer, with, they hoped, a ship full of furs. The first permanent base was at Three Saints Bay on Kodiak Island in 1784. It was eventually moved to Saint Pauls Bay on Kodiak Island. After Alexander Baranof arrived at Three Saints Bay in 1799, he developed a system of utilizing the Aleut hunters and their two-man biadarkas by recruiting them through dealing with the village chiefs. He sent these hunters out in the summer season in fleets of hundreds of biadarkas, accompanied by Russian supervisors in an armed ship, to protect the Aleuts from the fierce Tlingits. The hunters were paid at the end of the season for their share of the furs collected, and the village chief got his "cut" for providing the men and their biadarkas. By using this method of obtaining the furs, Baranof was able to control the procurement process, and did not have to compete with the other Russian companies or the English or American trading ships. His employees hunted for the sea otter and he paid them wages. As the Russians depleted the sea otter in the areas where they were first hunted, Baranof moved further south to his new base at Sitka, and even sent several hunting expeditions of Aleut hunters in their biadarkas, accompanied by an armed ship as far as California. The Aleuts paddled all the way down and back, often beset by storms which resulted in the loss of many men and their biadarkas.

Spaniards, next to arrive on the scene, were men and ships of the Spanish Navy, sent to explore and claim new lands, and did not engage in the fur trade. Spanish merchants did not try to enter the trade, either because they could not get permission from the government, because there wasn't much demand for warm furs in warm Spain, or because gold and silver mining in Mexico, the Phillipines, and South America was more attractive to them.

The only French penetration of this area, by LaPerouse in 1785, was similar to the Spanish, a naval expedition, and the only trading done was by the individual crew members. French merchants did not follow up on this voyage. They were undoubtedly fully occupied by affairs in their own country after the Revolution, and in European wars.

The first English exploration was that of Captain James Cook in 1778, again a naval voyage, and the only fur trading was by the individual crew members who, at that time, had no idea of the value of the sea otter furs that they acquired. They were merely looking for something to keep them warm when their ships penetrated Arctic seas. Though the crew did only a minimum of trading for sea otter furs, when that small number of furs arrived at Canton, China, the result was astonishing. The English and American merchants had no idea that these furs were extremely valuable on the Chinese market. The Russians already knew this of course, and had been trying to keep it a secret from the other Europeans.

Only a year after the first official account of Cook's voyage was published in London in 1784, the first English fur trader arrived at Nootka Sound. He was Captain James Hanna in the 60-ton brig *Harmon*. Hanna did not get off to a good relationship with the natives. When the Nootka chief, Maquinna, was visiting on board the *Harmon* they had Maquinna sit in a certain chair, a place of honor they said. After placing a small amount of "black sand" under the chair, and a thin trail of the same material leading away from it, they lit it and blew Maquinna right into the air. He survived, but later exhibited the scars as proof to the Spaniards. This affront to the chief may have been what prompted the attack on the *Harmon* by the Nootkas. Captain Hanna was able to repulse the attack, but only after considerable bloodshed. Eventually peace was restored, and trading continued.

This was only the first incident of mistreatment of the natives by the crews of English and American fur traders. As these attacks continued, the natives began to retaliate, capturing several vessels and massacring their crews.

Many more English ships arrived on the coast in the ensuing years. They all followed the original method demonstrated by Hanna, that of trading from their ships during the summer, and leaving for Hawaii and/or Canton in the fall and winter. They did not establish any permanent shore bases, which made them less vulnerable to attacks by the natives. The English traders concentrated their efforts in Nootka Sound, in British Columbia, and in Prince William Sound, and nearby Yakutat Bay in Russian America, as well as in Sitka Sound, before the arrival there of the Russians.

The American traders were not far behind the British. The first to arrive at Nootka Sound were Captain Robert Gray, of Columbia River fame, in the *Lady Washington*, a 60-ton ship from Boston, and Captain Kendrick in the *Columbia*, also from Boston, in September of 1788, only five years after the end of the Revolutionary War. Since most of these American fur traders were from Boston, all Americans came to be called "Boston Men" by the natives, conversely, their competitors, the British fur traders were known as "King George Men". Before long, the Americans overtook the British in numbers of ships arriving on the coast each year. As previously mentioned, most of the trouble between the natives and the white men was caused by these traders. In addition to abusing the natives, they sold them firearms and liquor, a deadly combination that often backfired on the white traders.

The American government did not send explorers to the area, they were too busy trying to put their new country together, and make it work after the Revolutionary War. All American action on the Northwest Coast was by private fur traders. The first government sponsored expedition to the Pacific Coast was the 1804-1806 overland journey of Lewis and Clark, who reached the Pacific Ocean at the mouth of the Columbia River on November 7, 1805, having come from St. Louis, Missouri, which they had departed on May 14, 1804. In 1806 Lewis and Clark made the return trip to St. Louis, arriving there in September. As word spread of the incredibly rich fur country that the explorers had found, a steady stream of trappers headed up the Missouri River the next spring, in 1807. The furs that drew these trappers west were those of the beaver. Beaver hats for gentlemen in Europe were the rage in the first part of the nineteenth century. As the trappers reduced the number of beaver in the middle west they pursued them to the west, to and beyond the Rocky Mountains.

The leading fur trader in the new United States, John Jacob Astor of New York, decided to take advantage of the information brought back by the Lewis and Clark expedition. In 1810 Astor formed the Pacific Fur Company and began a two-pronged effort, by land and by sea, to set up a fur trading post at the mouth of the Columbia River. The overland party was headed by Wilson P. Hunt, an American partner of Astor's, and the maritime venture was the *Tonquin*, a 300-ton vessel, commanded by Captain Johnathon Thorne, a former American naval officer. The *Tonquin* arrived off the Columbia first, and after some difficulty in crossing the bar at the mouth of the river, when two small boats and their crews were lost trying to guide the *Tonquin* across, they entered the river and by May 18, 1811, had completed a fort, which was named Astoria, in honor of the projector of the enterprise. After an arduous trip, the overland expedition arrived at Astoria a year later in 1812.

After the fort was built, the *Tonquin* departed on an ill-fated trading trip to the north. The ship entered Clayquot Sound, on the west coast of Vancouver Island near present day Tofino, and began to trade with the natives, who at first seemed to be very friendly, but soon swarmed over the *Tonquin*, killing all but four or five of the crew. The survivors barricaded themselves in a cabin and fired on the attackers. Realizing that they had no chance to retake their ship, they dropped out of a cabin window into the small boat tied alongside and beat a hasty retreat, but not before opening the kegs in the ships powder magazine, and lighting a fuse leading to it. As the natives looted the ship, it blew up, killing about 200 and seriously wounding many more. The survivors escaping in the small boat were soon overtaken and slain. The only survivor of the crew was a native interpreter who had been picked up earlier to assist in the trading. He escaped, and eventually made it back to Astoria, where he related the fate of the *Tonquin* and her crew. It was thought that the attack by the natives was in retaliation for the actions of another American trader who had recruited a dozen of the natives to assist him in a seal hunt, and, instead of returning them as agreed, had marooned them on an island off the California coast.

When the *Tonquin* did not return to Astoria, the traders at the fort realized that their means of communication and trading were lost. Their spirits were lifted however when a supply ship arrived in May 1812, the first of the ships that Astor intended to send out each year with supplies, and to return with furs. It appeared that Astor's project was a success, and that the American presence desired by President Jefferson in the Pacific Northwest had been established. This joy was soon dispelled, however, when in January, 1813, one of the partners returned from Spokane House, where a Northwest Company party of Canadian traders had told him that the United States had declared war on Great Britain, and that the War of 1812 was being fought. When the supply ship for 1813 did not arrive the Astorians thought it was because of a British blockade at sea, and that there would be no ships as long as the war continued. Astor's party at Astoria, believing that they no longer had a line of communication to New York for getting supplies, and the shipment of furs, decided to abandon their base at Astoria, and to return overland to St. Louis. The problem was solved for them when a party of 70 men of the North West Company, a Canadian firm operating out of Montreal, arrived and peacefully set up camp next to the fort. The two parties worked out a deal that was advantageous to both sides, the North West Company bought all of the buildings, supplies and furs of Astor's Pacific Fur Company on October 16, for $80,000, probably a very fair price at that time, especially since the Astorians would have abandoned most of it if they had departed, as planned.

The United States lost, at least temporarily, its only base on the Pacific Coast, but only for a few years. British gain of obtaining a Pacific Coast base peacefully was negated when, a month later, Captain Black of the Royal Navy sailed the *HMS Racoon* into the mouth of the Columbia River. His orders were to take the American fort. He was disgusted to see that a peaceful transfer had already been done, and decided to follow his original orders. He went ashore, raised the British flag, and took possession of the fort and the surrounding area in the name of King George. He named it Fort George. In this manner, a peaceful transfer was turned into an act of war, the consequences of which came into effect at the end of the war. The Treaty of Ghent ended the War of 1812 between Britain and the United States, which provided that each power return to the other any territory taken during the war. John Adams, the American negotiator, prevailed in his argument that this included the former Fort Astoria, so it was returned to American ownership. John Astor was not interested in returning to the Pacific fur trade, so the North West Company continued to trade at the fort it had purchased. In order to settle control of the Columbia River country, on October 20, 1818, Britain and the United States signed a convention that provided for joint occupation. This arrangement continued until 1846 when the Oregon Boundary Treaty was signed giving all of the area south of 49 degrees latitude, the present United States-Canada border to the United States.

The North West Company was one of two fur trading companies that controlled all of the fur trade in what is today Canada. It was a Montreal based company whose means of communication, with its far flung western trading posts, was by "brigades" of birch bark canoes from Montreal and the western forts , meeting at Fort William on Lake Superior in the spring, exchanging their respective cargoes and returning to their bases in the fall. They had penetrated most of western Canada, in fact, Alexander Mackenzie, whom we met in the previous chapter, was a North West Company partner. On his first overland voyage he reached the Arctic Ocean at the mouth of the river named for him. On his second journey, searching out new fur ground, and a possible route to the Pacific, he reached the Pacific Ocean near Bella Coola, British Columbia, on July 22, 1793.

The second British company was the much older Hudson's Bay Company which was established by King Charles II on May 2, 1670. Its charter gave it the sole right to trade in all of the country drained by rivers flowing into Hudson's Bay, known as Rupert's Land. Its headquarters were in London, and all decisions were handed down from there. Its first, and main base in North America, was at York Factory on the west shore of Hudson's Bay. For 249 years, until 1931, Hudson's Bay Company ships sailed from London to York Factory. Trading was first done only at York Factory, the natives bringing their furs down the rivers in their canoes. The company gradually expanded west, up the Nelson River to Lake Winnipeg, then up the Saskatchewan River, eventually all of the way to Edmonton, Alberta.

The Hudson's Bay Company had experienced competition from French fur traders operating out of Montreal, and operating up the rivers to the west, south of Rupert's Land. After the British defeated the French at the Battle of Quebec in 1759, Scottish traders replaced the French in the fur trade. The North West Company was one of the companies that emerged from the Montreal fur trade. Competition between the Hudson's Bay Company and the North West Company became very heated in the first part of the nineteenth century, and almost ruined the two firms. In 1821 the Hudson's Bay Company and North West Company agreed to a merger, and continued to operate under the name of the former company.

The Hudson's Bay Company had a greater impact on the history and development of the Inside Passage than any other institution, as we shall see. Like the Russian American Company, it was more than just a trading company. Since there was no established government of any sort in the entire area, just a number of independent Indian tribes, each ruling its own area and many of them in constant conflict, the Hudson's Bay Company became the authority, by default, if by no other way. They did not take sides in this intertribal warfare, but tried to discourage it. They would rather have the natives trapping furs than fighting each other. The Hudson's Bay Company always tried to stay on the best terms possible with the Indians and to treat them fairly in their trading with them, since they relied entirely on the Indians as the source for their furs, and as customers for their goods.

In 1825, the Hudson's Bay Company moved the site of their fur trading operation from Fort George, formerly Astoria, at the mouth of the Columbia to a new location 85 miles up river, six miles above the confluence of the Willamette and the Columbia Rivers. The new facility was called Fort Vancouver, and was dedicated on March 19, 1825, by Hudson's Bay Company Governor, George Simpson, on his first trip to the Columbia area, newly acquired from the North West Company. It was located on the north bank of the Columbia, near what is today the city of Vancouver, Washington, across the river from Portland, Oregon. The new location was more conducive to farming, and Simpson insisted that the establishment be more self sufficient in the matter of food supplies and not reliant on the extremely expensive method of bringing these supplies all of the way from London. Some of the men complained, saying that they were fur traders, not farmers, but Simpson prevailed, as he always did. Another change that Simpson made was to order that more coastal shipping be employed, both in bringing supplies from England, and returning the furs to London, as well as travelling the coast line, trading for furs, competing with the American traders who by this time had control of the trade. The North West Company had done nothing to foster the use of ships, even though Fort George was on the Pacific Ocean, preferring to use the overland canoe routes to Montreal. When the Hudson's Bay Company supply ship, *William and Ann*, arrived in the Columbia in 1825, she was sent north on a mission of fur trading and exploration for future expansion. She went as far north as Observatory Inlet and the Nass River, near the present Alaska-British Columbia border. The report was favorable, that furs were plentiful in that area.

Since the Hudson's Bay Company was planning to send ships and open up new trading establishments on the Pacific coast north of the Columbia River, they sought some help from their government in deciding the relative trading boundaries of the Russian American Company and the Hudson's Bay Company. The Russian and English governments drew up a treaty recognizing Russian sovereignty on lands north of 60 degrees latitude and west of 141 degrees longitude. In addition the area now known as the *"Alaska Panhandle"* was created when Russia was given that strip of land south of Mount Fairweather, as far south as 54 degrees 40 minutes, the present United States-Canada border, and extending inland ten leagues, about 30 miles from the salt water. The British would have use of all rivers right down to the salt water.

In 1827, the Hudson's Bay Company sent three ships north in the fur trade, the returned *William and Ann* and two small schooners, *Cadboro* and the *Vancouver*, the latter built at Fort Vancouver. The Hudson's Bay Company also erected a post at Fort Langley, at the mouth of the Fraser River. It was felt that the Fraser might be navigable for canoes from another Fort George, now Prince George, British Columbia, considerably shortening the overland supply route, and would also be removed from increasing threats from United States pressures on the Columbia, and the hazard of crossing the treacherous bar at the mouth of the Columbia would be avoided. Unfortunately the Fraser is not navigable, even for canoes, so Fort Langley did not become the replacement for Fort Vancouver as the main Hudson's Bay Company depot on the Pacific Coast, but it did remain as a trading post, and its farms important producers of agricultural products for the Hudson's Bay Company, and for salmon from the huge annual runs in the Fraser. Fort Langley was the first permanent European settlement on the Inside Passage, south of Sitka. Today, the present town of Langley, British Columbia, is a suburb of the city of Vancouver.

In March 1829, the returning supply ship, the *William and Ann*, was wrecked on the Columbia River bar. The ship was lost as was her entire crew and all of the supplies for the year for all of the Hudson's Bay posts west of the mountains. She was not the first, nor the last ship lost at this hazardous location, and pressure on the Hudson's Bay Company to find a better location for their Pacific base increased.

In 1830, the Hudson's Bay Company sent Aemilius Simpson north with three ships, the *Cadboro*, the *Eagle*, and the *Vancouver* to further investigate the Nass River area, and look for a site for a trading post. He picked up 200 beaver pelts in just two days of trading, and found a good site, but reported that American ships were active in the area and had driven up the price of furs. In April, 1831, Captain Simpson took the brig *Dryad*, along with the schooner *Vancouver* back to the Nass River. They arrived on May 11 and were warmly received by the natives. Once a new fort was built and was capable of defending itself, Simpson left on a fur gathering cruise. He became sick in the Queen Charlotte Islands, and returned to the new fort, where a doctor had been left. Simpson died shortly after returning to the fort and was buried outside the walls. The new fort was called Fort Simpson, in his honor. The site of the new fort was several miles up the Nass River, which soon proved too difficult and shallow for larger sailing ships to reach. Three years later the fort was moved to its present location on the Tsimpsean Peninsula, 18 miles north of Prince Rupert, British Columbia. It is now Port Simpson, a Tsimpsean Indian village, the oldest European settlement on the entire British Columbia coast north of Fort Langley on the Fraser River. Aemilius Simpson's remains were moved to the new location.

In 1833, the Hudson's Bay Company established two new forts along the coast as part of their expansion program. Fort McLoughlin was built a short distance south of today's village of Bella Bella and was strictly a fur trading establishment. Fort Nisqually was built at the mouth of the Nisqually River in southern Puget Sound, and, in addition to trading furs, had the mission of setting up farms and ranches to furnish food supplies for the northern posts that would be built. Its location was about eight miles southwest of present day Tacoma, Washington, and just off Interstate Highway 5 where the highway runs along the shores of Puget Sound.

In the spring of 1840, the Hudson's Bay Company peacefully took over Fort Stikine, on the Stikine River, near Wrangell, (Alaska of today), from the Russians. They also opened what was to be, briefly, their northernmost coastal outpost, Fort Taku, in Russian America, on Taku Inlet, just south of present day, Juneau, Alaska.

By this time, 1840, over hunting had almost exterminated the sea otter along the coast. For several years the Hudson's Bay Company fur trade had consisted almost entirely of furs brought down the rivers to the coast, primarily beaver, which had always been the mainstay of their trade in the interior, as well as furs of river otter, lynx, racoon and bear.

In 1836, the Hudson's Bay Company brought the *Beaver*, a side paddle- wheel steamer to Fort Vancouver. She was the first steamship to ply the waters of the North Pacific. She sailed from England around Cape Horn, and the two steam engines and paddle wheels were installed at Fort Vancouver. She departed Fort Vancouver on June 18, 1836, never to return to that location because she was too valuable to be risked in crossing the Columbia River bar. She had been brought to the coast because of her greater maneuverability and freedom from dependence on the fickle winds when entering inlets or traversing narrows, where currents often created problems. She proved to be a big success, the only drawback being that, since she burned wood as fuel, it was necessary to carry four stokers and 13 wood cutters on board, a great expense. She was valuable not only in easily reaching remote posts, but also was a big hit with all of the native tribes, who felt that she could do everything but speak, and that the white man must have been helped by the *Great Spirit* in her construction. The natives at Bella Bella were so impressed that they felt they must have one themselves, so they built one. They took a large cedar canoe, decked it over, built a cabin and smoke stack on it, and painted it, even to false gun ports on her sides. She travelled at all of three knots, and was propelled by paddles, the wielders of which were cleverly concealed by curtains on the sides. How useful the new *Beaver* was to the tribe was not reported. In addition to the *Beaver*, the Hudson's Bay Company had six large sailing vessels on the coast, all competing with the Americans. The Americans soon gave up the North Pacific fur trade because it was no longer profitable, due to the high prices the Hudson's Bay Company was paying for furs. As soon as the Americans were gone, the Hudson's Bay Company and Russian American Company cut their offering prices, for furs, in half.

In the spring of 1839, the Hudson's Bay Company in St. Petersburg, Russia, completed the transaction that would give it complete control of the entire Inside Passage. Governor Simpson of the Hudson's Bay Company and Baron Wrangell of the Russian American Company signed a ten year lease agreement for the coastal strip from Mount Fairweather, west of Glacier Bay National Park, south to Dixon Entrance, at 54 degrees 40 minutes. This lease also transferred the Russian Post at the mouth of the Stikine River, later Fort Stikine, to the Hudson's Bay Company. The Hudson's Bay Company undertook to provide the Russian posts with food supplies, ending their dependence on American ships and their own California post. With this lease, the Hudson's Bay Company controlled the entire Inside Passage, from Puget Sound to Glacier Bay and Skagway. Between the Hudson's Bay Company and the Russian American Company they controlled the west coast fur trade from the Columbia River to the western most of the Aleutian Islands. Working together they would drive the last of the

57

Americans from the coast.

Once the Hudson's Bay Company and the Russian American Company believed that the American traders would no longer be on the coast, and would no longer be competing with them by selling liquor to the natives, much to the detriment of the latter, they both agreed to halt the sale of this product. It was a great shock to the natives, since so many of them had become addicted.

In 1842, Governor Simpson ordered that, because of the success of the *Beaver* and the disappearance of the Americans, the northern posts were no longer needed, and all but Fort Simpson were to be abandoned. Trading henceforth would be done from the ships and transported to Fort Simpson or Fort Nisqually. In 1843, the Hudson's Bay Company made a major shift in their operations; they decided to eventually abandon Fort Vancouver, their main Pacific base, and replace it with a new fort to be built at the southern end of Vancouver Island, at present day Victoria. Two factors influenced this action, the first being continued losses and delays of their ships on the Columbia River bar, and the second was the increased encroachment of American settlers in the Willamette valley in today's Oregon. By the fall of 1843, Fort Victoria, as it was called, had been erected. On January 1, 1845, Governor Simpson ordered all furs to be collected at Fort Victoria, and all ships to and from England to use that port only.

On June 15, 1846, the United States and Britain signed the Oregon Boundary Treaty, and ended the joint occupation of the Columbia River Area. The international boundary was set at 49 degrees, an extension of the boundary that was in existence to the east of the Rocky Mountains. A jog to the south in the new boundary was included so that all of Vancouver Island, including three-year-old Fort Victoria, remained in British hands.

In May 1849, on orders from England, Fort Vancouver was shut down, and everything transferred to Fort Victoria. In the meantime, on January 13, 1849, the English Parliament had created the Royal Colony of Vancouver Island and leased it to the Hudson's Bay Company for an initial period of five years for an annual rent of seven shillings. The Hudson's Bay Company was to foster settlement of their new colony by bringing settlers out from England. If the Hudson's Bay Company had not fulfilled the requirements set forth at the end of five years, the colony was to revert to the crown and the company to be reimbursed for its expenditures on improvements. The factors influencing Britain in this action was fear of further encroachment by Americans, and to have some sort of administration set up by the Hudson's Bay Company. A royal governor, Blanshard, was sent out, but the real power remained in the hands of James Douglas, Chief Factor of the Hudson's Bay Company at Fort Victoria.

CHAPTER FIVE

MINERALS AND MINING

As we have seen in the previous chapter, it was the fur trade that first brought the attention of the Europeans to the North Pacific Coast, and the Inside Passage, but that impact was small compared to that of the discovery of gold in the area. The fur trade brought few outsiders to the area, as it was carried out by either the Hudson's Bay Company and Russian American Company through the small number of trading posts they established, or by traders in ships that made no settlements. In contrast, the Fraser River gold rush, in 1858, alone brought 25,000 to 30,000 gold seekers across Georgia Strait to that river valley in British Columbia in one summer, more men than had visited the entire North Pacific Coast since its discovery by Bering and Chirikov in 1741, 117 years earlier. These influxes of outsiders continued, off and on, for the next 40 years, culminating in the biggest gold rush of all, that to the Klondike, in the Yukon Territory in northern Canada in 1897. Many of these gold rushes were to places not located on the Inside Passage, but the Passage was the route traversed by the gold seekers on their way to the gold fields.

There was actually an earlier gold find in the Queen Charlotte Islands in British Columbia at Gold Harbour in 1850, but it was very short lived, because there was no gold in those islands other than the original small discovery. The rush to the Fraser originated when gold was discovered in the interior of British Columbia, near the junction of the Fraser River and its main tributary, the Thompson River, about 150 miles upstream from the mouth of the Fraser. Gold was first discovered by Indians, in 1856, who sold it to the Hudson's Bay Company at Fort Kamloops on the Thompson River. As the Indians, at the urging of the Hudson's Bay Company, gathered more gold and brought it to the company for sale, word of the find leaked across the American border, just one hundred miles to the south. Miners from what is now the states of Washington and Oregon began to push across the international border, illegally. They came overland, bypassing the Hudson's Bay Company posts at Fort Langley at the mouth of the Fraser River, and Victoria on Vancouver Island. In February 1858, Governor Douglas shipped 800 ounces of gold dust and nuggets to the United States Mint at San Francisco, the nearest point where gold could be marketed. This gold came from the Thompson River diggings. The population of Victoria paid little notice to the discovery, but when the shipment arrived in San Francisco, it produced an entirely different reaction. There were many men in California who had come west in the big California Gold Rush that began in 1849, and had little or no success. This news from British Columbia was just what they were waiting for.

On Sunday morning, April 25, 1858, an American wooden paddle wheel steamer, the *Commodore*, arrived in Victoria from San Francisco, and disgorged 450 passengers, who outnumbered the 300 residents of that settlement. Most of the passengers were miners, but some were merchants who came to set up businesses. There was no transportation available to the Fraser, as the Hudson's Bay Company ships were away, but the eager miners, undaunted, set out in canoes, rafts and small sailboats to cross Georgia Strait, and to start up the river. Ship after ship arrived all summer long, from San Francisco, most of them through Victoria, but some via Puget Sound ports. By the end of 1858, the population of Victoria had grown to 3,000, ten times that of the spring, and it had been transformed from a sleepy little English village to a bustling international sea port.

The miners found gold in the river's bars just below Fort Hope, 80 miles upstream from the Fraser's mouth, and continued working up river into the Fraser Canyon itself. The Fraser River gold was much easier to reach than that of the Thompson River, the miners could proceed all the way to the diggings by water, first by canoes, and a little later by paddle wheel steamers to Fort Hope, and eventually to Fort Yale, the head of navigation on the Fraser. By fall, several American paddle wheelers were allowed to carry passengers up river, to supplement the Hudson's Bay Company's *Beaver* and *Otter* which had been pressed into service. It was estimated that by the end of 1858, between 25,000 and 30,000 men had transited the river.

Since most of the miners were not British citizens, but citizens of the United States and European countries, something had to be done to preserve some law and order. James Douglas, Hudson's Bay Company's Chief Factor, and Governor of Vancouver Island, stepped in and, backed by marines and sailors from the Royal Navy's ships, did the best that he could. There were many problems because these were men fresh from the gold fields of California, where law and order were not the best, and the men were heavily armed as well. Douglas appealed to London for some assistance, because there was no recognized political entity on the mainland. It was just unorganized British territory. The result was that London revoked the Hudson's Bay

Company's ownership of Vancouver Island, but it remained a Crown Colony. A new Crown Colony of British Columbia was established on the mainland, and government officials for the new colony were sent from London.

James Douglas gave up his position as Chief Factor of the Hudson's Bay Company and was named Governor of both of the colonies; he had been governor of Vancouver Island since its inception as a Crown Colony. The Hudson's Bay Company's license of exclusive trade on the mainland was cancelled at the same time, bringing to an end its complete control over the entire Inside Passage. The Hudson's Bay Company continued in business over the area, but they now had competition, especially in providing for the requirements of the thousands of new miners going to the gold fields.

As more miners poured in, and the first diggings on the Fraser River bars were exhausted, the focus of the miners continued to move north, up the river. The finds became richer. In 1860, they fanned out into rivers to the east of the Fraser, into the area that became known as the Cariboo. By 1861, the big Cariboo Gold Rush was on, the biggest ever in British Columbia. The Cariboo Rush culminated at Barkerville in 1862 when Billy Barker, a Cornish sailor, and his partners dug down 52 feet until they reached the gravel of an old stream bed. They took out $600,000 of gold, worth about $20,000,000 today, and the biggest rush of all was on. Barkerville was soon the largest community on the West Coast north of San Francisco. The only trouble was that it was very difficult to reach. It was 400 miles from the head of navigation on the Fraser, Fort Yale, overland in very rough terrain. Wagon roads were eventually built, even through the vertically walled Fraser Canyon. To add to the difficulties, the Cariboo was snow covered for about six months of the year. In spite of all of these problems, thousands of gold seekers thronged through Victoria, and up the Fraser River. Evidently many of them had no idea of the hardships facing them when they left their homes. The Cariboo gold fields reached their peak by 1865, though they remained active for many more years. By 1865, they had produced about $22,000,000 worth of gold, which at today's values, is over half a billion dollars.

In addition to the effects on the coastal communities, the Cariboo Gold Rush opened up the interior of British Columbia for new settlers. In a few years, what is now British Columbia had gone from a trackless wilderness, populated only by Indian tribes, to a self-governing royal colony, with a legal system, a police force, and a rudimentary transportation system. A strange note is that the Hudson's Bay Company itself took no active role in this gold rush, acting only as a purchasing agent of the gold and as a supplier for the miners.

Several years ago, the Province of British Columbia purchased what was left of Barkerville, which had become a "ghost town", and restored it to the conditions existing at the height of its glory. Even though it is off the *"beaten path"* it is well worth a visit.

Gold was the mineral that had the greatest impact on the history of the Inside Passage, but it was actually not the first mineral to be found and mined. That distinction went to a much more mundane mineral, coal. Before coal was discovered in 1849 at Beaver Harbour, near today's Port Hardy on the north end of Vancouver Island, it was being shipped all the way from Wales at very high costs. Because of the high costs, the use of coal was mostly limited to the forges of blacksmiths, who could not get sufficiently high temperatures with wood. The discovery of coal came about when an Indian observed a blacksmith at the Hudson's Bay Company's Fort McLoughlin, near today's Bella Bella, about 80 miles north of Vancouver Island. When the Indian found out where the coal came from he said he knew where there were some of the black rocks a lot closer, near where he lived, in Beaver Harbour. The smith told him to bring some along in his canoe the next time that he came north. When he did the Hudson's Bay Company investigated, and finding the coal seam, brought some miners out from England as they doubted that the natives would make good coal miners. The Hudson's Bay Company used the coal for their own purposes at their forges, and converted the *Beaver* and their newer ship the *Otter*, from wood to coal for fuel. They also sold some to American steamers plying the waters of Puget Sound. The Hudson's Bay Company built Fort Rupert in Beaver Harbour to protect the miners, and serve as a fur buying location.

The coal was not of good quality and the seam was thin, but this problem was solved when better quality coal in larger quantities was found in 1852 at Nanaimo, on Vancouver Island, about 60 miles north of Victoria. Strangely, the find came about the same way as the earlier discovery, when an Indian was observing the smith at Fort Victoria, and said that he knew where there were plenty of those black rocks. He went home, loaded his canoe with coal and brought it to the fort. The Hudson's Bay Company transferred the miners down from Fort Rupert, and built a fortification, the Bastion, a wooden block house, which still stands on the hillside behind the harbor at Nanaimo. The coal fields at Nanaimo proved to be very productive, and became large producers of coal, continuing on well into this century. Coal was exported not only to Puget Sound, but also to San Francisco, which had also been dependent on Welsh coal. Coal was subsequently discovered at Bellingham and other parts of western Washington, creating competition for the Canadian mines, not only in the Puget Sound market, but also at San Francisco, which was the largest market.

During the last half of the 1860's and through the 1870's, there were many more discoveries of gold and other minerals along the coast of British Columbia as prospectors moved north. The coast mountains of British Columbia, Alaska and Washington are heavily mineralized, so good *"prospects"* as the miners referred to them, were plentiful, but none of them were major gold or silver discoveries until that of 1880 at Juneau in Alaska.

In October, 1880, an Indian guide led prospectors Richard Harris and Joe Juneau to the mouth of a small stream emptying into Gastineau Channel. Near the headwaters of the stream, they discovered a gravel deposit so rich with gold that they found it hard to believe. They staked their claims, as well as a 160 acre townsite for the expected rush, and returned to Sitka with the gold in their canoe, to record the claims. It was a fabulous strike, and prospectors poured into the region, though it was late in the season, and snow soon covered the basin where the strike was located. Since they could do no prospecting in the winter, the miners spent their time laying out the streets for a town and erecting a few crude cabins. In spring, the miners got to work on their claims in what was called Gold Creek valley. When regular steamship service from San Francisco, Portland, and Victoria was inaugurated in March, 1881, the new camp became very easy to reach, compared to other gold discovery camps. You could take a steamer right to the gold field. Just five months earlier, the only transportation available to Juneau and Harris was by dugout canoe and paddles from Sitka.

Mining was done at first by the old Placer Mining Method, with a gold pan or a rocker and sluice. No one got terribly wealthy, but it was a good start. In the first year $80,000 to $100,000 in gold was taken out, worth about 25 times more in today's dollars. Underground, lode mining was the answer, but it took more work, equipment, and especially capital, so was slower to develop.

The first big lode, or underground mine, in the area, was not in Juneau, as the first settlement was called, after one of its founders, Joe Juneau. It was across Gastineau Channel, on Douglas Island. John Treadwell bought a lode claim on the island for $400 in 1881, and wasn't too excited about it until he saw the assay report on the 22 sacks of ore he took to San Francisco. On his return, he bought some adjoining claims, and, in 1882, brought a five stamp mill to process the ore. Within two years 120 more stamps were added.

The stamp mills were composed of huge metal slabs that crushed the ore so that it could be sent to a smelter that would produce the finished product, pure gold. By 1889, the Tacoma Smelting and Refining Company built a smelter on the shores of Commencement Bay, in present day Tacoma, Washington, and began smelting, in addition to the gold ore from the Treadwell Mines, silver, lead, and later copper. In 1905, Tacoma Smelter and Refining was taken over by American Smelting and Refining Company, ASARCO.

The Treadwell mines continued to grow, and dominated Gastineau Channel for 35 years. The town of Douglas was created to house employees of the mine and mill, and eventually equaled Juneau in size. The Treadwell alone employed 1,200 people.

Mining was first carried on in a huge open pit, which eventually reached 450 feet in depth. Later, mining was done by shafts, which reached as deep as 2,400 feet. At the height of operations there were four adjoining mines at Treadwell, the Treadwell, Ready Bullion, Alaska Mexican, and the Seven Hundred Foot Mine.

A huge cave-in on April 22, 1917, allowed sea water to rush into and flood three of the mines, sparing only the Ready Bullion, which was separated by a bulkhead. Miraculously, no lives were lost, but all of the horses and mules used in the mines were drowned. The Ready Bullion continued mining for another five years, but the other three mines were destroyed permanently. Within a year the population of Douglas dropped by 75 percent.

Two large mines on Mount Roberts, the site of the original Harris-Juneau strike, kept the city of Juneau going after the demise of Treadwell. The first was the Alaska Gastineau Mining Company that began operations in 1915 and ran until 1921 when it became unprofitable and shut down. The second mine was the Alaska Juneau Mining Company known as the A-J. The A-J mill opened in March 1917, and operated until April 9, 1944, when mining in Juneau ceased, 64 years after the original strike. The ruins of the A-J mill still loom on the mountainside above the city, reminders of Juneau's origin.

Juneau was named the new capital of Alaska in 1900 to become effective as soon as adequate buildings were provided, taking over from Sitka. This occurred in 1906 when the newly appointed governor, Wilford Huggat, took office. By the time the mines and mills shut down, government had become Juneau's main business, as it continues to be to this day.

Gold was never Alaska's most valuable resource, but it did accomplish one thing, it brought the territory to the attention of the citizens of the United States, and, in fact, of the civilized world, when the rush to Juneau got under way. The other thing that the Juneau strike did for Alaska was to give it a transportation system for the first time. Previously, there had been only a monthly steamer from Portland to Sitka since the purchase of Alaska by the United States in 1867. During 1881, a stream of ships from San Francisco, Portland and Victoria arrived bringing miners to the new goldfields, known as the Juneau Gold Belt, which stretched from Berners Bay 35 miles northwest of Juneau to Windham Bay 60 miles southeast. For the first time, scheduled transportation along the entire thousand mile long Inside Passage was available, except for the hundred miles that remained from Juneau to what was to become Skagway.

The biggest gold rush of all along the *Inside Passage* started in mid July, 1897, when two ships from Alaska arrived at San Francisco and Seattle. The *Excelsior* was the first to dock, at San Francisco, on July 14, 1897. The miners staggered ashore under their loads of gold, and headed for the Selby Smelting Works. The United States Mint was closed. Their gold was in suitcases, boxes, packing cases, bottles, cans, and every type of package imaginable. A crowd of people followed, and watched as the gold was dumped out on the counters. Word spread through the city and made the headlines of the local newspapers, as well as being spread nationwide by the wire services. The scene was repeated in Seattle when the steamer *Portland* docked there a few days later at 6 a.m. on July 17. News of the *Excelsior*'s cargo had come from San Francisco, so 5,000 people were on hand to greet the miners disembarking from the *Portland*. One Seattle paper, *The Post Intelligencer*, issued three extras that day stating that one ton of gold had come off the *Portland*. The rival *Seattle Times* was more conservative, making it half a ton. For once they both underestimated, as the total was close to two tons of pure gold, not gold bearing ore.

The *Excelsior* and the *Portland* had both come from St. Michael, Alaska. Their passengers had arrived there from Dawson City, Yukon Territory in Canada. They had made the trip from Dawson City to St. Michael, a 1700 mile voyage down the Yukon River on small paddle wheel steamers as soon as the ice cleared from the river in the spring. Prospectors had been working the area around the site of Dawson City for some years, but most activity had been concentrated around *Fortymile*, farther down the Yukon in Alaska. Gold had been found around Dawson, but nothing spectacular. This was to change on August 17, 1896, when George Carmack and his two Indian friends, Skookum Jim and Tagish Charley, struck it rich on Rabbit Creek, a tributary of the Klondike River, which, in turn was a tributary of the mighty Yukon. Later, Rabbit Creek's name was appropriately changed to Bonanza Creek and a tributary was named Eldorado. To the outside world, the whole area became known as the Klondike. The three men were actually looking for a good place to cut some timber which they intended to raft down the Yukon to the trading post at Fortymile, in Alaska, and sell it. They had been doing some prospecting as they went along, struggling through the mosquito infested underbrush. According to history, Carmack picked up a thumb-sized nugget of pure gold from a protruding rim of rock, and then panned some gravel, which returned about four dollars worth of gold. Since a ten cent pan had been considered a good prospect, this was incredible, and they knew that they had struck it rich at last. No more wood cutting for them. They staked four claims, two for Carmack, the discoverer, as allowed by law, and one claim each for Skookum Jim and Tagish Charley. They did not realize it, but they were standing on some of the most valuable ground in the world, gold was all around them, and it was pure gold nuggets, not gold ore that required milling and smelting. Leaving Jim behind to guard the claims, Carmack and Tagish set out for Fortymile to record them. As was customary in the gold fields, the two men spread word of their discovery as they met other prospectors, who immediately took off to stake their own claims. When Carmack told his story at Fortymile all of the old timers laughed at him, as he was known as a great braggart,

"*Lying George*", but when he showed them his nuggets they stopped laughing and headed up the river. The rush to the Klondike was on, but it did not become a "*stampede*" until the arrival of the *Portland* and the *Excelsior*, and word spread to the rest of the world.

The first ship north was the *Al-ki*, which sailed from Seattle on July 19. One thousand people were on the dock to wish the 110 passengers "bon voyage". In addition to her passengers there were 900 sheep, 65 cattle, 30 horses and 35 tons of supplies; there was not an inch of space left unoccupied. When the *Willamette* left Tacoma on August 7, 7500 people were there to watch her leave with 800 passengers, 300 horses and bales of hay stacked so high on deck that forward view from the bridge was obstructed. Every ship going north was similarly overloaded, because space was at a premium, to say the least. Few of the ships heading north to the Klondike gold fields bothered with safety precautions, and the living conditions aboard were indescribable, many passengers comparing them to the infamous Black Hole of Calcutta.

In the first five weeks after the arrivals of the *Portland* and the *Excelsior*, 20 steamers left the Pacific Coast for Alaska. Every available ship was pressed into service, and retired ships and ships abandoned on the beach were "*refurbished*" and added to the fleet. Anything that would float was filled with anxious passengers and freight. Capable officers and crews were scarce, so it is not surprising that there were many accidents and ship wrecks. The Inside Passage is one the most difficult and dangerous waterways, even for sound ships and qualified officers and crews. Even so, there were many more people seeking passage north in the summer of 1897 than there was available space. Newspapers, the publicity men of the Pacific port cities, railways, steamship lines, outfitters for miners were all shouting the praises of the Klondike and urging men to go there and make their fortune. A few voices were counselling caution, but no one heeded them. In August, the United States Secretary of the Interior, C. N. Bliss, issued a warning against trying to reach the Klondike that season, because it was already too late in the year. The Canadian Minister of the Interior had already published a similar statement, but both fell on deaf ears. Louis Sloss of the Alaska Commercial Company which was going to benefit from the stampede stated that, "I regard it as a crime for any transportation company to encourage men to go to the Yukon this fall." Few listened; by September 1, 9,000 people and 360 tons of freight had left from the port of Seattle alone.

Why did the Klondike stampede reach such intensity, out of all proportion to the amount of gold that really existed in those gold fields? There had been recent rushes, to California, South Africa, and Australia, where the fields were much richer, but they did not create the frenzy that equalled that of the Klondike. The answer is that conditions were ripe for this lunacy, for that is what it was. The world was at peace, there were no rivals for public attention. Both Canada and the United States were suffering from a long, deep depression, and there existed, for the first time, plentiful cheap transportation to the west coast in the form of the several new transcontinental railways in the United States and one in Canada. A railway fare war erupted that saw the fare from Chicago to the west coast drop to $10 for a while. The Pacific Coast ports in the United States and Canada put on extensive advertising campaigns, each trying to lure prospective miners to travel through their port, and most important of all, to buy their outfit and supplies there. Most of these promotions made thoroughly false claims to incite more "*stampeders*". They exaggerated the amounts of gold and how easy it was to be found and also how easy it was to reach the Klondike. Although few would believe it, there was by this time no chance that any traveller would reach the Klondike before the following summer.

Seattle received, by far, the biggest share of the Klondike trade, five times as much as all of the rest of the ports put together. It was not by accident, as they spent five times as much on paid advertising as well as a huge amount of free advertising, largely as the result of press releases generated by the secretary of the advertising committee, Erastus Brainerd, who eventually took his own advice in the spring of 1898, and left for the Klondike himself.

There were several different routes that the miners used to try to reach the Klondike. The route the majority used, in the late summer and fall of 1897, was that of the Inside Passage, by steamers or various other types of vessels to either Dyea or Skagway, the twin settlements in Taiya Inlet at the head of Lynn Canal, in Alaska, 100 miles north of Juneau, and 900 miles north of Seattle. There were no settlements, so tent cities sprang up, soon replaced by crude log huts. There were no piers or other port facilities so ships were forced to anchor a mile off shore. Passengers had to go ashore and transport their gear on rafts or scows to shore, where it piled up, much of it to be ruined when high tide arrived. The livestock were merely dropped overboard and forced to swim for it.

Once ashore, the really difficult part of the trek began. It was still 500 miles to the Klondike, and the first thing that had to be overcome was the mountain range that rings the head of Taiya Inlet. There were two choices, the Chilkoot Pass, above Dyea, or White Pass, above Skagway. The Chilkoot Pass was the established route, and is the best known, if for no other reason than the photographs that most readers have seen of the solid line of humanity, forming a black line against the huge white mountain wall that rose 3,500 feet above sea level. The last four miles were the worst, with a grade of 30 percent and the last half mile, 35 percent. This pass was shorter than the White Pass route, but 600 feet higher, and much more difficult. Nevertheless 22,000 people had crossed Chilkoot Pass by the spring of 1898, according to the records kept by the Mounties at the top of the pass, the international border between the United States and Canada. The Royal Canadian Mounted Police were stationed at the border in February, 1898, to keep law and order, which was sadly lacking in Alaska, and to deny entrance to anyone who did not have the approximately 1,200 pounds of food and supplies which they considered to be essential for survival for one year. A customs house and inspector were also located at the summit to collect the duty due on non-Canadian goods that were being imported. The Chilkoot Indians, both men and women, took advantage of the situation by working as packers. Rates started at 5 cents per pound, but quickly went to 40 cents, when the rush was on. In the spring of 1898, an aerial tramway 14 miles long carried freight all of the way to the summit. Dyea and the Chilkoot were not to continue in use much longer. During the winter of 1898-99, a narrow gauge railroad was built over White Pass above Skagway. Most of the stampeders, who crossed the Chilkoot during the winter months, were subject to brutal weather. Heavy snows, of almost 70 feet, fell on the Chilkoot summit during the 1898 season, and there were strong cold winds from the interior. One result of the heavy snowfall was a huge avalanche that occurred Sunday, April 3, 1898. It covered ten acres to a depth of 30 feet. More than 60 people died in the avalanche, only a handful were rescued alive.

From the Chilkoot summit it was a drop of 1,200 feet in a little over 10 miles to Lake Lindeman, one of the headwaters of the Yukon River itself.

Undoubtedly the main reason that so many of the miners chose the Chilkoot that year was that the heavy snows had closed the White Pass for the winter. The closing of the White Pass route resulted in an increase in the population to about 5,000 at Skagway until it was reopened. Dyea did not experience such growth, because traffic continued to move over the Chilkoot all winter long, with several interruptions because of snow storms.

With 5,000 migrants temporarily stranded in Skagway, and no law and order, it was a scene ripe for crime and misdeeds of every sort. That is exactly what happened. By midwinter, Jefferson Randolph Smith, better known as "Soapy" Smith was the dictator of Skagway. He held the power of life or death over everyone in Skagway and along the trail to the Canadian border, where the Mounties had placed Maxim machine guns to protect the border. He had the militia and the local law enforcement agencies in Skagway either cowed, or in his pay. His methods were as varied as extortion, robbery, and rigged gambling establishments. His spy network, which he used to spot potential "pigeons", stretched all of the way back to Seattle and Victoria, on the numerous steamers. He had learned his trade in the mining camps of Colorado: Leadville, Creede, and Denver. When he learned of the Klondike strike, he set out for Seattle and eventually Skagway, with five of his principle henchmen, to be the nucleus of his infamous organization. His control over Skagway continued until July 8, 1898, when he and Frank Reid, who was heading a vigilante group formed to stop Smith's actions, killed each other in a confrontation. Smith died immediately and Reid, the hero of Skagway, died a few days later. A new deputy marshal was sworn in and the vigilantes rounded up the ringleaders of the Smith gang, including the corrupt marshal. The new marshal, at considerable danger to himself, prevented any lynching of the gang members, who were put on steamers to Sitka and Seattle where they were tried, convicted, and given jail sentences. With Smith and his gang gone, Skagway and Dyea settled down to some semblance of law and order.

In 1897, most of the Klondikers crossed the passes too late in the fall to continue on to Dawson. The lakes and rivers were frozen just as the authorities had predicted. Only a very few people were able to float down the Yukon to Dawson before freeze-up. The rest settled down on the shores of Lakes Lindenman and Bennett, to wait for the ice to go out so that they could continue on their way to Dawson. They spent their time constructing all sorts of craft that they hoped would take them there.

Some 10,000 people spent the winter and spring on the shores of Lake Bennett alone, and a total of 30,000 were strung out from Lindeman to Tagish Lake. Superintendent Samuel Benfield Steele of the Mounted Police, the same man who set up inspection points at the two passes, and his men kept things orderly in this mob. Handguns were prohibited in Canada, and were confiscated by the Mounties, to be returned when the owner departed Canada. This served to stop the shootings which had previously been everyday occurrences. This ban on handguns still exists throughout Canada. Steele not only protected the stampeders from the criminal element, but also from themselves. His men went through the camps observing the boat building, and made suggestions about safety and durability of the craft. He also had the builders of the boats put a serial number on each of them. These were recorded, along with the names of the occupants and addresses of next of kin. These lists were sent to police posts along the river, and, if a boat failed to check in, the Mounties searched for it. As a result, the unruly flotilla of over 7,000 boats made the dangerous 500 mile trip with only a few fatalities.

The ice began to break on the lakes on May 29, and the great boat race was off. Within 48 hours, all of the lakes were clear and 7,124 boats loaded with 30,000 stampeders and 30 million pounds of food and supplies were on their way. The going was easy until the voyagers left the lakes and entered the Yukon River where they had to run through Miles Canyon near Whitehorse, Yukon Territory, and the rapids below it. Most of the stampeders were not experienced boatmen, and had little knowledge of what lay ahead of them. In the first few days 150 boats were wrecked and five men drowned. This created a traffic jam as several thousand craft lined the banks above Miles Canyon, their captains unsure of what to do. Sam Steele came to the rescue again, when he and his men arrived on the scene. He set up rules, (1) no women and children to go through on the boats, and (2) no boat will be allowed to go through the rapids until Corporal Dixon, an experienced river man is convinced that it has sufficient free board to ride the waves safely, and (3) that it has a capable steersman and crew. The corporal was the only judge of whether a craft met the standards, and a $100 fine was assessed if the rules were broken. As a result, the wrecks and deaths nearly ceased. Of the 30,000 who floated down to Dawson that summer, there were only 23 drownings, much to the credit of the Mounties who shepherded them from checkpoint to checkpoint. With the rapids behind them, the voyage down the Yukon became a race to get to Dawson ahead of the crowd, and to stake a good claim. The few remaining hazards were navigated with relatively few wrecks, thanks to the help and advice of the Mounties who were stationed at each of them.

Boats started trickling into Dawson at the end of May, but it was not until June 8 that the first part of the main fleet arrived, pouring in, day and night, filling the shore line until there was no more room. Late arrivals had to tie to earlier boats. The boats were soon six deep for a two mile stretch along the shore. Boats kept arriving for another month, and steamers coming up the Yukon from St. Michael, Alaska, brought still more people and freight to Dawson. In one month, it had become the largest city in Canada west of Winnipeg and only slightly smaller than Seattle, Tacoma, or Portland. It was much larger than Vancouver or Victoria. The Mounties estimated Dawson's population that summer at around 18,000, with another 5,000, or so, out in the remote mining areas.

As the thousands milled about Dawson and the mining camps, they began to realize that few of them were going to get rich. The best claims had been staked long ago, probably before these people even left Seattle or San Francisco. Gold nuggets were not laying on the ground, waiting to be picked up, as many had imagined. Many of the disillusioned stampeders found work in the existing mines, in the numerous business establishments that sprang up, or in erecting the buildings that housed them. By July 1, Dawson City had two banks, two newspapers, five churches, and numerous hotels, stores, saloons and gambling and dance halls. It is estimated that by the end of the summer of 1898, one third of the stampeders had left Dawson and the Klondike, most on one of the 60 steamers that had made the trip and then returned to St. Michael.

Dawson was a much more peaceful town than were the Alaskan towns of Skagway or Dyea, thanks again to the Mounties. Handguns, illegal in Canada, were confiscated if found. Not a single murder took place in Dawson City in 1898, and very little major theft.

Most of the 650 arrests made in the entire Yukon in 1898 were for misdemeanors such as fraud and disturbing the peace. Of the 150 more serious offences, more than half were for prostitution. This is not to say that everything was open and above board in the operations of the Yukon government, because it was not. Most of the problems occurred in the office of the Mining Records, where claims were recorded. There bribery, corruption and general inefficiency were common. Examples would be the changing of names or dates on claims, long delays waiting in line to transfer claims while others, who had greased a palm, were taken care of first. Another fraud was to tell a potential claimant that the ground was closed by the government, then later allowing a friend or briber to register on that claim. All in all it must be said that the lives and property of the miners were much more secure in the Canadian mining camps than they would have been in any of the American camps of that period.

A great surprise to most of the newcomers to the Yukon was the strict observance of the Sabbath. Not only were the saloons and dance halls shut down at exactly midnight, Saturday, but no work of any kind was allowed on Sunday, and they meant any kind. One man was arrested for sawing his own wood, another for fishing and according to a newspaper report of August, 1898, two men were fined $5 each for merely examining their fish nets. It is not hard to imagine the amazement of men and women, who had come through Skagway and Dyea; talk about culture shock!

The route over the passes and down the Yukon was not the only way to reach the Klondike, but it was the one used by the great majority of the stampeders. It was made much easier when the White Pass and Yukon Railroad was completed to the summit of White Pass on February 20, 1899, and to Lake Bennett on July 6. In the following year, in July, 1900, it was completed to Whitehorse, but the great Klondike gold rush was over by then.

The easiest way to reach the Klondike was by the all-water route called the "Rich Man's Route". This was by steamer from a Pacific Coast port to St. Michael, Alaska, near the mouth of the Yukon River, then 1,700 miles up the river on a paddle wheel steamer. No walking or climbing, and your baggage came with you. The only problem, in addition to the cost, was that the river was frozen solid for six months of the year, which few of the stampeders realized. In the fall of 1897, 1,800 Klondikers started on the all-water route, but only 43 reached Dawson before winter, and 35 of those arrived without their outfits, which they had thrown away in their desperation to arrive before it was too late. When freeze-up came many people were caught on steamers in the ice along the 1,700 mile route. Initially there was a great shortage of transportation on the river, but that was eased when 30 new steamship companies came on the scene in the summer of 1898, in addition to the original two. During that summer there were sixty voyages to Dawson, but by that time it was too late; the Great Gold Rush to the Klondike was over.

There were several overland routes that both American and Canadian stampeders used to avoid each other's country and its problems, such as duties. All met with disaster. Many of these men were city dwellers with no outdoor experience and no idea of the difficulties that faced them. The Americans were lured by tales of the "All American Route", with no Canadian customs duties to pay. One route was overland from Valdez, in Prince William Sound, Alaska, to the interior rivers. They first had to cross the Valdez Glacier, in winter, not really knowing where they were going. Blizzards, avalanches, and snow blindness plagued them on the glacier, and they became lost in the interior. It is estimated that less than one half of one percent of the 3,000 who tried this route ever reached the Klondike. A smaller number, the total is uncertain, tried to cross the huge Malaspina Glacier at the head of Yakutat Bay, Alaska, with no better luck, meeting incredible conditions on the huge icefield.

The Canadians promoted several "All Canadian" overland routes, avoiding American customs at Skagway, Dyea, or St. Michael. Several thousand people tried these routes, with no better success than their counterparts on the "All American Routes". One route, known as the "Ashcroft Trail" ran 1,000 miles north from Ashcroft, a settlement 125 miles northeast of Vancouver, British Columbia, to the Yukon. There was no real trail at all, and the terrain, mountainous and heavily wooded, was almost impossible. At least 1,500 men and 3,000 horses tried this route, and only a handful reached their goal. Another Canadian route was that of the Stikine River, which met the Ashcroft Trail at the river port of Glenora on the Stikine. Men who used this route met with more success than those coming all of the way from Ashcroft, but still met with great difficulties. In the spring of 1898, there were 5,000 people massed in Glenora waiting to set out on the trail.

The most misled groups of all were those who attempted one of the several overland routes from Edmonton, Alberta, varying in length from 1,500 miles to 2,500 miles, lured on by the merchants of Edmonton who tried to convince the world that their city was the only practicable gateway to the Klondike. Sam Steele of the Mounties thought that it was "incomprehensible that sane men would attempt any of the overland routes from Edmonton", but several hundred did. Most of them spent two winters on the trails; a handful made it, arriving in August, 1899, after it was all over. As far as can be determined only three of the handful that made it ever found any gold. Most of the survivors took the next boat out.

It is estimated that about 100,000 stampeders set out for the Klondike during the years that the stampede lasted, and around 30,000 to 40,000 actually reached Dawson City. Only about half of this number actually looked for gold, and only about 4,000 found any; a few hundred in large enough amounts to call themselves rich. Out of these fortunate few, only a handful managed to keep their wealth very long.

Dawson's end came as swiftly as its birth, when word spread up the Yukon River of a tremendous discovery of gold on the beaches of Nome, Alaska. Like rats leaving a sinking ship, 8,000 people went down the Yukon in a single week in August, 1899, bound for the new gold fields. It was the same old story all over again, a rerun of 1897-98. The same week a few of the survivors who had set out from Edmonton two years earlier straggled into Dawson, the last of the *"stampeders"*, there were no more. Dawson's period as a *" metropolis"* had lasted just 12 months, from July, 1898 to July, 1899.

The great "Klondike Stampede" was one of the strangest and most useless mass human migrations in history; the rewards hardly equalled all of the money spent, and, as we have seen, it was very unevenly distributed. On the bright side, the stampede left some permanent benefits. It opened Alaska, and the Canadian northwest to the rest of the world. The great strike at Nome, short-lived as it was, was followed by many more across Canada and Alaska. Many returning stampeders settled down on their return to careers as farmers, loggers, fishermen and business men in the northwest. The new hoard of gold reaching the market ended the gold shortage and tight money that had created the depression of 1893. Half a dozen west coast cities owed their growth to the stampede: San Francisco, Tacoma, Portland, Vancouver, Victoria, and most of all, Seattle. Dawson did not disappear as some mining camps did, it just shrank to a small permanent population and huge Placer mining dredges worked over the old claims in the creek valleys as big business took over from the small independent miners.

The Nome Gold Rush, which began in July, 1899, was different from the Dawson City rush in several ways. The gold that first drew prospectors was in the sands of the ocean beaches that were easily processed by a lone miner with a pan or a rocker to wash the sand and recover the gold. Later finds were located a bit farther inland, in old shore lines, created when the sea level was higher, and in the beds of some of the creeks that ran into the ocean. Secondly, it was easy to reach by taking a steamer directly to Nome, and coming ashore on a barge or small boat. The ships had to anchor offshore. Nome has never had a real sea port, because it is shallow off the beaches and no piers or wharves have been built. The winter ice and storms would tear them out every year. Thirdly, it is a truly god-forsaken location, permafrost is a few inches under the surface of the ground, meaning that it remains frozen all year. There are no trees for many miles, and the ocean is frozen for six months of the year. Lastly, it is in Alaska, not the Yukon, and all of the lawlessness typical of American mining camps prevailed; no Mounties were on site to preserve law and order. Nome was the biggest Alaskan gold rush.

About 30,000 prospectors rushed to Nome as soon as the ice was out in the spring of 1899. The rush lasted only three months, however, because it was ended by a tremendous storm in September, when winds up to 75 miles per hour and towering waves destroyed the town and all of the beach mining operations. Before the Pacific froze over, half of the stampeders, (15,000 of them) were gone. They didn't want to spend a winter in Nome. In spite of its poor location, Nome has survived, and today is a city of about 5,000 people. It is the transportation, supply and government center in Northwest Alaska.

Nome was the last of the big gold rushes that swept through regions along the Inside Passage. However, the search for, and exploitation of, mineral resources by no means stopped in 1900, at the end of the nineteenth century. In fact, it was just getting started. The Coast Mountain Ranges of Washington, British Columbia and Alaska, and the offshore islands, which are really drowned mountains, are all very heavily mineralized, and the nineteenth century gold rushes alerted the geologists and prospectors of the world to this fact. In addition to gold, subsequent exploration and mining has located, and in most cases eventually exhausted large deposits of coal, silver, copper, lead, iron, zinc, molybdenum, uranium, asbestos, marble and jade. Many of these mines were adjacent to the waters of the Inside Passage and the communities that sprang up around them created considerable traffic at times. Presently there is very little mining going on along the coast, although a great deal of activity continues in the interiors of British Columbia and Alaska.

When approaching Juneau, ruins of the Alaska Juneau Mine are seen on the eastern shore of Gastineau Channel.

CHAPTER SIX

SEWARD'S FOLLY? THE PURCHASE OF ALASKA

When Alexander Baranov, the so-called *"Lord of Alaska"* departed Sitka in 1818, he could never have imagined in his wildest dreams that in less than 50 years, his beloved territory would be sold by the Russians to the United States, but that was exactly what happened in 1867. Thirteen governors followed Baranov at Sitka, mostly naval officers and other men of rank. They were responsible men, and performed their duties well, but none could match his drive.

The idea of selling Russian America, as it was then called, to the United States first came up in 1854, when Russia was on the brink of entering the Crimean War against England, and realized that they were too weak to defend their North American colony if it was attacked. Nothing came of this overture, but the Americans were interested. Britain had no designs on Russian America and was glad to sign an agreement that they would not molest the colony if the Russians would agree to leave the Hudson's Bay Company alone.

After Russia's disastrous defeat in the Crimean War, Russian morale was very low, and they needed money to pay their war debts. Recalling the interest shown by the United States in a purchase of Russian America in 1854, St. Petersburg ordered their American Ambassador, Stoeckl, to see if there was currently any interest in a purchase, but before any progress could be made the United States Civil War erupted, ending the negotiations. In 1866, after the Civil War was over, St. Petersburg called Ambassador Stoeckl home, and instructed him to begin talks on the sale again, for not less than $5,000,000. Russia never looked for other buyers, there probably weren't any.

William H. Seward, the American Secretary of State, was the man with whom Stoeckl would have to negotiate. Seward was Lincoln's

Secretary of State through both of his terms as president, and had continued in that position under Lincoln's successor, Andrew Johnson. Seward was an ardent expansionist, and Stoeckl knew that he was anxious to have Russian America for the United States. Seward was also anxious to get the sale completed quickly, as the Senate, which would have to approve the purchase, was scheduled to adjourn at the end of the month of March, 1867. Seward did not wait to get President Johnson's approval, but began negotiations on March 14 with an offer of $5,000,000, which he immediately raised to $5,500,000 without even waiting for an answer. By March 23, the main points of the purchase had been agreed upon, and Stoeckl had pushed the price up to $7,000,000, the maximum that Seward was authorized to pay. Stoeckl received approval on March 29, and added some minor changes, which Seward turned down, but countered by raising the price to $7,200,000. After two copies of the agreement, one in English and one in French were drawn up, Seward had them signed at 4 a.m. on March 30, much to the amazement of Stoeckl, who was not accustomed to such hurried proceedings.

Seward had the Senate's session extended for the needed approval and finally succeeded in getting approved by only one vote over the necessary two-thirds of the total votes. The United States had acquired 586,400 square miles, twice the size of Texas, for less than two cents an acre. Seward could probably have made a better deal if he had not been in such a hurry.

It took 15 months to get the House of Representatives to pass an appropriations bill to pay Russia, but that was finally done in June, 1868. There was approval of the purchase by a large segment of the public and the press, but there was also a great deal of disapproval. Many people had no idea where Alaska, as it was now called, was, or what it was like. Critics said that it was worthless because it was frozen over all year long. Terms such as *"Seward's Icebox"* and *"Seward's Folly"* were applied to the new acquisition. As we all know now, it was a great bargain, and has paid for its cost many times over. A few years later Seward was asked what he considered the most significant act in his career. He declared without hesitation, "The purchase of Alaska, but it will take the people a generation to find that out."

At Sitka, on October 18, 1867, as Russian and American cannon fired a salute, the Imperial flag of Russia came down, and to the continued salute the Stars and Stripes were raised. And so, 126 years after Bering's discovery of the region, and 68 years since the founding of the Russian American Company, Russian rule was over.

At the time of the transfer, the future for Alaska, and Sitka in particular, looked promising, and businessmen arrived from San Francisco anxious to share in this new opportunity. The future for the remaining Russians, those who were not government or naval personnel, was not too dark either, as they were given three years to decide whether to stay or get free transportation back to Russia. Individuals would be given title to buildings and land that they occupied and all facilities for carrying on trades and professions would also be made over. It looked like a "can't lose" arrangement; they would be working for themselves instead of the company, and could leave if it did not work out. For the United States, the treaty of cession provided that on the part of the United States, all inhabitants remaining, with the exception of the "uncivilized natives", would enjoy all of the rights and privileges of citizens of the United States.

Alas, things did not turn out as hoped for, mainly because the United States Congress, which had never been too enthusiastic about buying Alaska in the first place, turned its back on its newest "child", and for the next 17 years left it without any government, legal system, or laws of any sort. Instead of doing what was expected of it, providing a territorial government, with a civilian governor, a legislature, courts, and appropriate laws, Congress made Alaska a customs district, and left it at that. William S. Dodge, the United States Customs Officer, was the only government official, and he had nothing to work with. For the first ten years, until 1877, Alaska was put under military occupation, because the United States Army was given control and 500 troops were stationed at Sitka and Wrangell.

The military rule was not good, because the troops were undisciplined, and allowed to carouse, loot, and rape at will. The treatment was so bad that nearly all of the Russians packed up and left, as did most of the Americans. Without some sort of government, and legal system, no one was legally entitled to settle, buy or sell, or take title to property.

There was one successful business venture, however, that of the Alaska Commercial Company, a San Francisco venture that for $350,000 bought all of the assets of the former Russian American Company at Sitka, Kodiak, Unalaska, and the Pribilof Islands, and some remote trading posts. The Pribilofs up in the Bering Sea, were the main attraction for the new company as they were the summer breeding grounds of the Alaska fur seals. The Russian American Company had been taking these furs for some time, and the new company intended to continue that practice. By stepping into the shoes of the Russian American Company, the new company continued to provide some order in the area where they were operating, in the Pribilofs and Aleutians, but the rest of Alaska was not doing so well. The Army withdrew in 1877, when they were needed to help put down an uprising in Idaho and Montana by the Nez Perce' Indians. The only government officials left in all of Alaska were Montgomery P. Berry, the customs collector at Sitka, his deputies and three postmasters, and some Treasury agents in the far away Pribilofs.

As glad as the citizens of Sitka were to see the unruly army troops depart, they were concerned about protection from the Tlingits, who were their neighbors. Illegal alcohol was freely available and, when consumed by both the white and Indian inhabitants, resulted in frequent disturbances. Several citizens wrote letters to Washington requesting some sort of protection. In response, the Navy sent the United States gunboat, *Alaska*, north from San Francisco. The British Navy was the first to arrive, however, as some of the population had given up hope of ever getting any response from Washington, and had written to the authorities at Victoria, which sent *HMS Osprey* to the rescue. The *Osprey* stayed until the *Alaska* finally arrived ten months later, on April 3, 1879. The United States Navy took over and for the next five years the government of Alaska was in their hands. The Navy operated with no more legality than had the Army, because there was still no government structure or legal system, they could only make the best of it, but it was more orderly.

Congress finally did what it should have done 17 years earlier, when on May 17, 1884, they passed the Organic Act of Alaska. While not ideal, it was a beginning. It placed the territory under the civil and criminal laws of Oregon. It created a governor and officials to handle legal matters. A great deal of the credit in getting Congress to finally move must go to a Presbyterian missionary, Dr. Sheldon Jackson, who arrived on the scene in 1877, the year the Army pulled out. While engaged in his missionary activities, Dr. Jackson realized the sad state of affairs that existed in the territory, and the need for changes. Through lecture tours throughout the United States, and with the help of groups he organized in churches, Congress was made aware of its negligence, and that some sort of governmental system must be provided. That finally happened on May 17, 1884, four years after the discovery of gold at Juneau, and the ensuing rush of miners. This should have been enough to alert Washington that Alaska did have some value, and should be given some consideration; but it took Dr. Jackson and his followers to do the job.

Alaska finally gained territorial status in 1912, and on January 3, 1959, it became the 49th state of the Union.

CHAPTER SEVEN

THE FORESTS

From Washington, through British Columbia and into Alaska, the most conspicuous feature of the Pacific Northwest, that meets the eye of a newcomer to the area, is the forests. The forests that we see today are second and third re-growths, and though still impressive, they are only a faint imitation of the original, old growth forests. These forests have been the single most valuable resource of the Inside Passage. Timber has been, and still is the leading industry in the British Columbia and Alaska sections, and, until recently was also the number one industry in the state of Washington.

The few remaining stands of old growth trees are mostly remote and seldom visited by travellers. The largest trees along what is now known as the "Inside Passage" were the Douglas Fir, the Sitka Spruce and the Western Red Cedar. They were huge. Most important, the Douglas Fir, averaged around eight feet in diameter and over 200 feet in height, and the others were not far behind. It is not hard to imagine the impression that these huge trees, larger than any previously seen, made on the first European explorers, who saw an endless source of masts and spars, as well as shipbuilding materials, and made use of them to repair their well worn ships.

The natives, of course, were the first people to make use of the forest's resources, primarily the Red Cedar. The cedar trees provided the natives with logs needed to make the hulls of their dugout canoes from small one-man craft to the largest, over 30 feet in length, capable of carrying a large crew of fishermen, hunters or warriors. The natives also used the trunks of the cedars for the huge beams in their "long houses" and split planks from the cedar logs, with crude tools of stone, wood and bone, to cover the sides of the big buildings. Wood was also used to fabricate tools, weapons, utensils, boxes, and was woven into hats and clothing. Totem poles were carved from whole trees.

The first European and American settlers put little value on the forests, other than as a source of local building materials. Often they were seen as a hindrance to erecting buildings, creating towns and farms, and road construction. This changed when they realized that there was a very large export market waiting to be supplied. The first sawmill in the area was erected at Tumwater, on Puget Sound, near today's Olympia, Washington. It was a mill that the Hudson's Bay Company had used at Fort Vancouver on the Columbia and was sold, when replaced by a newer mill. The output of this mill went to local consumption, most of it to the Hudson's Bay Company for their farms around Fort Nisqually.

In 1848, the Hudson's Bay Company built a sawmill on Vancouver Island, at Millstream, near Fort Victoria, again for local consumption, but when the 1849 gold rush in California occurred, nearly all of the lumber was shipped to San Francisco for use at the gold fields.

The Oregon Boundary Settlement of 1846, ceding all of the territory south of latitude 49 degrees, by Britain to the United States, opened what is now Washington to settlement by United States citizens. The first settlers came to the area around today's Olympia, and in the fall of 1851 a small group came to Alki Point to begin what has become Seattle. In 1852, the settlers moved to a site on Elliott Bay and began building. In 1853, Henry L. Yesler built a steam sawmill to provide lumber for the new settlement. The first shipment of timber occurred the previous year when a ship from San Francisco showed up to see if anything was available, and bought logs that the settlers had cut down in clearing the land.

The first large scale, well financed lumber operation in the Puget Sound area was started by two lumbermen, from Maine, Andrew Pope and William Talbot. They had come to San Francisco to establish a market for their Maine mills, but soon realized that this would be even more futile than "carrying coals to Newcastle". The California gold rush of 1849 had created such a demand for lumber, primarily for use in sluices to carry water to the diggings, that one New England ship that brought miners out to California had built berths for its passengers from hemlock that had cost $10 a thousand board feet, and ripped out the boards and sold them for $300 a thousand in San Francisco. Demand was so great, and supply so short, that in addition to the considerable amount of lumber being brought from Maine, all of the way around Cape Horn, a voyage of five or six months, some was also being imported from Norway, Australia, and Chile. It didn't take long for these shrewd Yankees, looking around at the greatest forests in the world, to realize that this was truly a golden opportunity awaiting them. They had the "know how", the capital, and the equipment and ships. All they had to do was move it out to the West Coast and go to work. They decided their headquarters would be in San Francisco, and that they would look to the north for their mill site and timber supplies. They were not interested in the tremendous forests on the northern California and Oregon coasts because there were no good ports available. The only safe havens were Humboldt Bay in California, or the Columbia River. Both had treacherous bars that must be crossed in entering. These men were also very experienced mariners with many of their own ships, and they wanted a safe, secure harbor, approachable at all times. For these reasons they decided to investigate the Puget Sound area, about which very little was known in San Francisco at that time. In fact, one ship, the *Kendall*, had been sent to Puget Sound for the purpose of bringing, in 1851, ice back to San Francisco from the glaciers that the owners were certain must be there. After all, it was at the same latitude as Newfoundland, which had plenty of ice. They found that the Sound, like the rest of the Inside Passage, was ice free all year long, so settled for a load of pilings from the trees cut down by the first settlers at Seattle, as they cleared land for their settlement. Pope and Talbot decided that Puget Sound would be their timber source. Pope remained in San Francisco to handle the marketing, while an associate, Captain J. P. Keller, went back to Maine to fetch the needed sawmill equipment, as well as the Pope, Talbot, and Keller families.   Talbot set out for Puget Sound in the *Julius Pringle*, another vessel they had acquired, and eventually found just what he was looking for on the east shore of Hood Canal, an inlet off Puget Sound. The harbor, which was named Port Gamble, is about 20 miles northwest of downtown Seattle of today. In 1853, the new mill was in operation and Pope and Talbot's Puget Mill Company was in business. So began one of the most successful, long-lived, forest products firms in the northwest. It was the first fully integrated operation, owning its own supplies of timber, operating the latest efficient sawmills, owning their own ships, and marketing, in many locations, through their own lumberyards.

Being canny, experienced New Englanders, they were well financed, and avoided the heavy debt loads that plagued many of their local competitors. Around their mill, they built a town for their employees that was a replica of a New England coastal village, even to the maple shade trees that were brought out as seedlings. The village of Port Gamble has been preserved in its original state, and is well worth a visit if one is in the area. As the firm grew, it expanded to another operation in nearby Port Ludlow.

The loggers first cut those trees that were closest to the salt water, and rolled them into the water, where they could then be towed to the mills, also situated on the water's edge. As the supply of trees along the shore lines was exhausted, some method of retrieving trees growing farther inland and transporting them to the mills after they were cut was needed. These were huge trees, and were very difficult to move once they were felled, trimmed, and cut into shorter lengths. At first, teams of horses and oxen dragged them to the water's edge.

81

The next step was building "skid roads" out of logs to make it easier to move the logs. A later development was the "donkey engine", a stationary engine, originally powered by steam. By means of a cable and drum the logs were pulled to water. Gasoline, then diesel engines replaced steam as power, but the "donkey engine" is still in use today. As it became necessary to go farther afield for more timber, logging railroads were built and operated for many years. A few logging railroads are still in operation, but the majority of logs are transported by trucks today. Many logging companies have built their own private roads, where they are not subject to the size and weight limitations of public roads, and can operate larger, more efficient units. In both British Columbia and Alaska, the latest method of getting trees out of the forest is by helicopter, because logging has proceeded up the mountain sides onto steeper terrain. This method eliminates both the cost of road building, and the considerable damage done by the construction of these roads. In many areas, this is the only type of logging allowed by the Forest Services.

Logging has progressed from a very labor intensive operation to a highly mechanized one today, the result being that fewer and fewer loggers are putting out more and more lumber. The sawmills have also become larger and more efficient as improvements in equipment have been made.

The logging sites were usually some distance from the saw mills, so the logs had to be transported to the mills. The salt water provided the easiest way to move the logs. This was done by forming the logs into large rafts, which were then towed by one or more large tugs. During the 1980's some of the British Columbia logging firms began to use "log ships" instead of rafting. The log ships load the logs by huge cranes mounted fore and aft on their hulls. The logs are stacked crosswise on the ship's decks, and are unloaded by flooding water compartments on one side of the ship, causing it to list, or tilt, sufficiently to make all of the logs slide off into the water. At first, the log ships were towed by large tugs, which could tow their ship-shaped hulls much faster and more efficiently than they could tow the log rafts. In recent years, some of the new log ships are self-propelled, and do not need tugs. Both methods of moving logs are in use today, and log rafts and ships are a common sight along the Inside Passage.

Another recent change in the logging industry has been the shipment to Japan and other Asian markets of whole, un-milled logs. Some of these logs are loaded on ships from docks, but most loading is done by towing the logs to the foreign ships, and letting them bring the logs aboard with their own cranes.

For a long time, the timber industry concentrated on only providing logs for sawmills, and marketing the output of the sawmills; boards and timbers. As the industry matured, it broadened its scope to other fields. The most important of these new areas has been the paper pulp industry which now produces a large part of the total revenues of these companies. Along the Inside Passage, there are large pulp mills, all the way from Tacoma and Everett on Puget Sound, to Ketchikan and Sitka in Alaska.

Until the discovery and exploitation of the great forests in the northwest, the primary source of timber for the United States markets had been the forests of the upper Midwest, in Michigan, Wisconsin and Minnesota. Rapid harvesting of these forests was fast depleting them, and it became obvious that new sources of timber would have to be located. At about the same time, when the Northern Pacific Railroad was completed from Duluth, Minnesota to Portland, Oregon in 1883, and the Great Northern Railroad connected Minneapolis and Seattle in 1893, the Pacific Northwest obtained improvements in transportation facilities connecting to the eastern states. This newly available rail transportation to eastern markets greatly increased the prices that northwest lumber would bring, and the lumber companies took advantage of this and began shipping large quantities of lumber by rail. The Lake State lumbermen, by far the largest firms in the country, saw the opportunities also, and acquiring large tracts of timberland in Washington, moved their operations west. The greatest of these was Frederick Weyerhauser, who for many years had dominated the lumber trade east of the Rocky Mountains. In 1900, he purchased 900,000 acres of timber land from the Northern Pacific Railroad Company, land that the federal government had given the railroads to entice them to build the roads. He formed the Weyerhauser Timber Company, whose holdings had increased to 1,500,000 acres by 1905. Weyerhauser Timber Company has their headquarters in Tacoma, and has become the world's largest timber operation.

Let us turn our attention to forests a bit farther north, those of the Canadian province of British Columbia. These forests are British Columbia's single greatest resource, yet, at first, they were not considered to be of any great value, just something impeding the progress of settlements and road building; and the Hudson's Bay Company, the early authority, was anxious to have as much cut as possible. The first sawmill in British Columbia predated even that of Yesler in Seattle in 1853. James Douglas, of the Hudson's Bay Company, had a mill constructed at Millstream near Victoria, on Vancouver Island in 1848. During its first year, the output was used locally in construction, but with the surging demand for lumber at San Francisco after the gold rush of 1849, the lumber was shipped there because it would bring a much higher price. Whole logs, which were used for pilings, and required no mill work, were shipped to San Francisco from Sooke, Vancouver Island in 1852.

Canadian firms began logging the forests on the shores of Burrard Inlet, site of today's Vancouver. First shipping spars and pilings in the 1860's, with the establishment of the Hastings Mill in 1865, they began turning out finished sawed lumber. It was shipped to San Francisco at first, and later to Latin America, Australia, China, and even to Britain.

British Columbia, which had been a Crown Colony since 1858, joined the Canadian Confederation in 1871 when it was promised that, if they joined, a transcontinental railroad would be built, joining it to eastern Canada. Eastern Canada dragged their feet in performing on their promise, and this railroad was not completed until 1885. Granted, it was a tremendous undertaking for a country as sparsely populated as Canada was at that time. At any rate, The Canadian Pacific Railroad reached Burrard Inlet in 1885, and a new city, Vancouver, sprang up. The railroad had an immediate effect on the hitherto virtually unpopulated Canadian prairies as farmers and ranchers rushed in and towns sprang up along the railroad route. British Columbia forest industries took advantage of this new market, and the new means of transportation to reach it, and began to expand, shipping lumber there as well as to eastern Canada, which was now more accessible.

The opening of the Panama Canal in 1914 opened even more markets for all Pacific Coast lumber, and growth of the industry continued. Much of this growth came from the expansion of American firms into British Columbia as timber stands in the United States became scarce and more expensive. In 1910, investment in the British Columbia forest industry was about two million dollars, all of it Canadian. By 1920, the total investment had grown to $65 million, 90 percent of it American. With the infusion of American capital and experience, the forest industry boomed.

After 1896, the forested lands of the province were not sold outright, but were leased to logging firms. Today, the government of British Columbia still owns 95 percent of the province's forests. Of the remaining five percent, some has been sold and some given as incentives to railway builders, as was done in the United States.

During the early years of the twentieth century, changes occurred in the forest products industry. Lumber produced by the sawmills became a less important factor in the whole industry as new plants produced plywood, which was becoming an ever more important building material, and pulp mills produced newsprint, as the rapidly growing United States market clamored for more of that product.

At first, the timber industry was not interested in the forests of Southeast Alaska along the northernmost reaches of the Inside Passage. They were too far from the markets of those days, making the shipping costs prohibitive, and labor costs were higher. Even farther-north Alaska could get lumber shipped from the Lower 48 cheaper than from Southeast Alaska.

Alaska's first sawmill was built in 1879 at Shakan on Kosciusko Island, about 50 miles southwest of Wrangell. It produced lumber for local construction and for cases to ship the canned salmon from the canneries that sprang up about that time. Other small mills came into existence in the 1880's at Metlakatla on Annette Island and at Dolomi on Prince of Wales Island, 15 miles south and 25 miles southwest of Ketchikan, respectively. They only produced for the local market. This was the beginning of the timber industry in Alaska, but it was years before further development began.

As World War II became imminent, the demand for Sitka spruce for use in the construction of the British Mosquito bombers soared, and continued to the end of the war. Southeast Alaska and British Columbia have the world's greatest stands of Sitka Spruce, and their timber industries benefitted from this sudden spurt in demand, that died with the end of the war.

The production of wood pulp for the manufacturing of newsprint has developed and sustained the forest products industry in southeast Alaska. The first pulp mill was built at Ward cove on the

northern outskirts of Ketchikan by the Ketchikan Pulp Company in 1954. It was the largest non-military construction project in Alaska to that time. Logs to supply this mill came from the Tongass National Forest on Prince of Wales Island, across Clarence Strait from Ketchikan. The forest products industry, including the loggers and workers in the pulp mills, became, by far, the largest employer in Southeast Alaska, and has continued to be so to the present time.

Local Campbell River cabinet maker carved statue of high rigger for pole commemorating the timber industry.

85

CHAPTER EIGHT

THE FISHERIES

The fishing industry is one of the most important segments of the economies along the entire Inside Passage, and has been for a long time. In fact, as we saw in earlier chapters of this book, it was the abundance of food supplies from the seas that encouraged the first humans to settle here, ten thousand years ago.

The ocean waters teem with fish, not as plentiful as one hundred years ago, but still present in respectable numbers. The marine animals that are taken by the fishing industry can be divided into two main categories, fin fish, and shell fish. The fin fish category can be further segregated into those fish that are usually found at or near the surface, and those found at or near the bottom.

The five species of salmon are surface, or near surface dwellers, and are economically the most important fish. These species are the (1) red or sockeye salmon; (2) the Chinook, king, or spring salmon; (3) the coho or silver salmon; (4) the pink, or humpback salmon; and (5) the chum or dog salmon. Even though they are distinct, separate species, they have certain common characteristics. They are hatched from eggs deposited in gravel beds of fresh water streams, and as small fingerlings swim down stream, often hundreds of miles to the saltwater, where they spend two to five years, until as adults, they return to the same stream where they hatched, spawn, and then die. The length of time spent at sea depends on the species. The pinks are two year fish. The other four species spend from three to five years in salt water, roaming the open seas, before returning to their stream of birth. The pink salmon are the most numerous of the species, and the smallest in size, adult fish weighing from three to six pounds at maturity. The Chinook are the largest salmon, averaging from 15 to 30 pounds, though some individuals have weighed more than 120 pounds. Chinooks bring the highest prices per pound. The sockeye, or red salmon are small fish, weighing about four to seven pounds, and are usually the species with the highest total market value. The coho is also a commercially valuable salmon and is the one usually taken by sports fishermen, who put great value on its fighting ability. The adult coho weigh from four to 16 pounds.

Chum salmon are usually considered to be the least desirable of the species. They are sold either in the canned form, or frozen, but are really best when smoked. The advent of fish farming or aquaculture, has brought a sixth salmon species to the west coast, the Atlantic Salmon. The first fish farms in British Columbia were established by Norwegians, who had pioneered this method in their homeland, where the Atlantic Salmon is the native fish. Because they were familiar with these fish, they continued to use them in their British Columbia farms, and this practice continues today.

Commercial fishing for salmon, as well as for other fish, was at first slowed by the great distances between the fishing grounds and potential markets. Consequently, early efforts were confined to the local, relatively small, fresh fish markets. Salting was the method used first to preserve salmon for the export market. This technique dates back as far as the days of the Hudson's Bay Company, which began salting Chinook salmon only, in the late 1820's, at first on the Columbia River, and later on Puget Sound and the Fraser River in Canada, and shipping the product to Hawaii, Australia, China, England, and markets on the east coast of the United States.

The salmon saltery was eventually displaced by the cannery, which opened a world wide market to the salmon of the Pacific Northwest. Canned salmon had a wider appeal to the public, than did the taste of the salt salmon, which sometimes arrived in less than prime condition. The first canneries on the Inside Passage were established in 1870 on the Fraser River, near Vancouver, British Columbia, and on Puget Sound, in 1877, in Washington at Mukilteo, north of Seattle. Canning the Pacific salmon began on the Sacramento River in California, when the Hume brothers, salmon canners from Augusta, Maine, built a very small salmon cannery in 1864 on the banks of the Sacramento River, near the village of Yolo, just north of Sacramento, California. The Chinook salmon were the only salmon canned in this first cannery. In 1866 the Hume brothers, looking for *"greener pastures"* built the first cannery on the Columbia River, 40 miles upstream from Astoria, at the mouth of the river. This cannery prospered and the Humes built several more, as did other early entrepreneurs. By 1881, there were 35 canneries strung along both banks of the lower Columbia, with the Hume brothers founders of at least half of them. The

Chinook was still the only salmon that these early canneries were processing.

The fishermen of Puget Sound and the Fraser river soon adopted this new and better method of preserving salmon for the market, and built canneries. This opened a huge new market for the product, and new canneries were built on the British Columbia coast to the north. By 1901 there were 70 canneries between the Fraser River on the south to Portland Canal at the Alaska border to the north. Today there are only about a dozen still operating, all concentrated in Prince Rupert or in the Vancouver area. At one time there were 17 canneries operating in Rivers Inlet alone, today there are none. The entrance to Rivers Inlet is 65 miles north of Port Hardy, which is the north end of Vancouver Island. After the Fraser and the Skeena rivers, Rivers Inlet has the third largest salmon runs of British Columbia. The demise of the coastal canneries occurred because of modern methods of refrigeration and freezing, which made possible the transportation of salmon catches to the central points of Vancouver and Prince Rupert for canning.

The canning business was necessarily a very seasonal and labor intensive affair, which made it necessary to transport many workers up the coast and back each year. This was very expensive. It was cheaper to bring the fish to the laborers than vice-versa. The canneries used as many of the local Indians as employees as they could attract, but it was necessary to bring in many more laborers, most of them Asians. When the season's pack was over, the canneries were shut down, leaving only caretakers, until the following year.

The first canneries in Alaska were built at Klawock, on the west side of Prince of Wales Island, and at Sitka in 1878. In a little more than a decade, the industry spread north all the way to the Bering Sea. At one time in the 1920's, 25 salmon canneries were operating on Prince of Wales Island alone. Ketchikan, which billed itself as the "canned salmon capital of the world", had 13 canneries in 1940.

Over the years, fishermen have used several methods of taking salmon. The natives, the first fishermen, were the smartest, because they knew that the salmon would come to them. They used dams and traps to take them in the rivers and streams on their annual return to spawn. The white men used traps for a while, but outlawed them in British Columbia, Washington, Oregon, and California after salmon runs began to decline. It was because the traps were too efficient. They were not forbidden in Alaska until it became a state in 1959. The no-trap ban was one of the first acts of the new legislature.

Today, salmon are taken commercially by various types of boats and methods. Before the invention of the internal combustion engine, the power was either sails or oars, and the craft were necessarily quite small. The advent of first the gasoline and then diesel engines, for boats, made the fishing process much more efficient, increasing the catches of the individual fishermen. In order to control the number of fish taken each year, the Canadian and United States governments have instituted licensing to limit the number of commercial fishing boats, and have restricted open seasons for additional control.

There are three methods of taking salmon commercially today. Trolling is the simplest, and similar to the one used by most sport fishermen. The boats used are the smallest of the commercial boats, usually 25 to 35 feet long, with a one- or two-man crew. Trollers were originally powered by oars or sail, but converted to gasoline engines when they became available. They can be identified by the two or four long poles that are carried in a vertical position when not engaged in fishing, and lowered to a 45 degree angle when trolling. Lines with hooks and lures, bearing weights to take them to desired depths, are suspended from the poles. The lines are hauled periodically, and fish removed. Although trollers are numerous, their catch is a relatively small portion of the over all catch.

Another method of fishing is gill netting. The boats used are a little larger than the trollers, about the same 25 to 35 feet in length, but wider in the beam. One or two usually suffice for the crew. The nets are up to 1200 feet long, about 30 feet deep, supported by a string of floats, and are weighted on the bottom so that they hang vertically in the water. They are deployed in a more or less straight line, across the areas where the salmon are expected to travel. The nets are hauled every one to four hours by a power drum, on which they are stored. The salmon are taken when they swim into the net, and are caught by their gills, becoming trapped in the net mesh. A large red float marks one end of the net, and the boat the other end. Gill netters often work in large fleets, and can be a hazard for pleasure boaters. They avoid setting their nets in lanes used by larger boats, such as cruise ships, ferries and freighters, because these vessels are not maneuverable enough to avoid the nets.

The purse seiners are by far the largest commercial fishing boats used on the Inside Passage, ranging from 40 to 100 feet in length and carrying crews of four to eight men. The seines, or nets, are about 1200 feet long and 60 to 70 feet deep. When a school of fish, hopefully salmon, is located on the sonar, the net is set. One end is attached to a skiff. That small boat runs in a circle, deploying the net, hoping to set it around the school of salmon; the other end of the net remains attached to the seiner. The net is supported by floats, and held in a vertical position by weights at the bottom. If the set works, the salmon are now *"fenced"* in. Next the *"purse"* is closed by pulling on the line which runs through metal rings on the bottom of the net. Finally the seine and the fish are hauled aboard the big seine boat. Purse seining accounts for the largest portion of salmon taken commercially, because it is, by far, the most efficient method.

Since 1980, fish farming, or aquaculture, has come on the

scene. Salmon are raised in net pens supported by rafts. They are fed pellets tossed into the pens. Aquaculture has been around for years in Norway, whose coastline is very similar to that of the Inside Passage. The Norwegians raise the Atlantic salmon, which are the native fish in their waters. Fish farming has been so successful, that in 1996 half of the salmon sold on the world's markets were farm raised fish. The fish farming industry has grown not only in Norway, but also in Chile and along the Canadian and United States coasts of the North Atlantic Ocean.

Success in replenishing the stocks of salmon produced in fish hatcheries has also increased, resulting in larger runs of fish returning to the rivers. The results have been a glut of fish on the market, and a consequent severe drop in the price of salmon caught by the fishing fleets. This price drop has been reflected in prices at the super markets; and often fresh or frozen salmon are the lowest priced fish offered. The fish farms of the Inside Passage are primarily in British Columbia. The British Columbia government encouraged their growth with low cost loans or guarantees for loans, because their economy was depressed during the 1980's, and this was a new industry to spur growth. It has succeeded, after a few false starts, but at the expense of the commercial fishing industry. In an attempt to protect their salmon fishermen, Alaska has forbidden the establishment of salmon farms. They have not done well in the state of Washington, either because of stringent regulations or water conditions, or both.

The second most important fishery along the Inside Passage is the herring fishery. Herring are small fish, eight to ten inches in length, that mature and spawn in three years. They are a very important food source for other fish, especially the salmon. Herring roe is a valuable product and is taken in two ways, one of which is, directly from the fish which are taken by purse seiners. After the roe is removed, a small amount of the herring is processed in various ways: fresh, smoked, canned, or salted, but most of the fish are reduced to fertilizer. Another method of taking the herring roe is to harvest the kelp fronds on which it collects. This is considered a delicacy in Japan, as is all herring roe, and Japan is the principal importer for these products.

Another very important fish in the Northeast Pacific Ocean fishery is the halibut. They are not taken any longer commercially in the waters of the Inside Passage, but are in the offshore waters of Alaska, British Columbia, and Washington. Sports fishing for halibut, however, is very popular in the inner waters.

The first commercial halibut fishery, in 1888, was around Cape Flattery, Washington, at the western opening to the Strait of Juan de Fuca. It was *fished out* in a few years, and the halibut fishermen looked north, both in the protected inside waters and out in the Pacific. As they fished out one area, they moved north. In the early 1890's, methods of icing halibut for the long railroad haul east began to be used. The

90

demand for this excellent fish grew, and more fisherman went after halibut. Before World War I the coastal fishery for halibut was abandoned as unprofitable because the catch numbers had dropped dramatically. The only place left was the open waters, deep seas fishery. That was where most of the halibut had always been. Numbers eventually began to drop because of the heavy fishing pressure, but the United States and Canada, the only two countries involved, ratified a halibut conservation treaty on March 2, 1923, and began to place limits on open seasons. Halibut stocks have gradually increased. Today the problem facing the halibut fishery is the presence of the foreign trawl fleets that drag their nets along the bottom, taking many young, immature halibut along with the other fish.

The halibut is a strange looking fish, a "flat fish" that spends much of its time resting flat on the bottom of the sea. The bottom side of the halibut is white, and the top side is a dark, mottled brown. Its two eyes are both located on the dark upper side. When the larvae are hatched, the eyes are on opposite sides, as on most other fish, and when the fish is less than in inch long one eye begins to migrate to what will become the dark upper side. At four to six inches in length, the juveniles settle to the bottom, where they remain for the rest of their lives. Halibut grow slowly; it takes about five years to reach a length of around 20 inches. A mature male will weigh from 50 to 100 pounds, while a fully grown female may be more than eight feet long and weigh 500 pounds or more at about 15 years of age.

The commercial method used to take halibut is called "long lining" and consists in using hundreds of baited hooks tied to a heavy, long line strung along the bottom and held in place by weights. The hooks are placed about 20 feet apart and a long line set is about 18,000 feet or a little over three miles long. This makes for about 900 hooks per line. The boat then sets other lines, of the same length, about a mile apart, parallel to the first line. The lines are left on the bottom for about 24 hours before they are hauled, and reset. The lines are set in several hundred feet of water. They are brought into the boat by power winches, and the halibut removed and stored in an ice filled hold for transport to Prince Rupert, Vancouver, or Seattle for processing.

Various other types of fish are taken commercially along the Inside Passage, but not in quantities of any importance. These include various species of rockfish, often sold as "snappers", flounders and sole, ling cod, and true cod.

SHELLFISH

Several species of shellfish are taken commercially, or raised in aquaculture farms along the Inside Passage, though not in numbers to

91

equal the values of salmon, halibut or herring. Several types of shrimp are taken, some by trawl or drag nets, and some by the use of baited traps, or "pots". Nets are used where the bottom is smooth enough to prevent damage to the net, and pots are used where the bottom is too rocky or uneven, which is true for much of the Inside Passage.

The Dungeness crab is the most important crab taken commercially, and is found all along the coast, especially in bays and inlets because it is a shallow water resident. They are taken by the use of baited traps or "pots".

The King crab is much more important commercially, but few are taken in the Inside waters; the bulk of the fishery is in the deep waters of the Gulf of Alaska and the Bering Sea, in some of the roughest waters in the world.

Oysters, various species of clams, and mussels are taken commercially in the waters of the southern end of the Inside Passage, Puget Sound in Washington, and Georgia Strait, between Vancouver Island and the mainland in British Columbia, because they need warmer water. Many of these shell fish are farm raised, on floating rafts or on the bottom, and harvested when grown to market size.

The cannery and reduction plant buildings of Butedale Cannery still stand. Once one of the most important canneries on the coast, it has been in-operable since the 1950's.

CHAPTER NINE

TRANSPORTATION AND COMMUNICATION

Transportation and communication are always a very important element in the history of a region, and this is especially true of a remote, unexplored territory like the Inside Passage.

TRANSPORTATION BY WATER

The oldest forms of transport were the cedar canoes of the natives. Because of the nature of the terrain, there were few trails, and most of them led into the interior. The easiest way to get from one village to another was by water, and this is still true today. Along much of the British Columbia and Alaska coast, roads are very few and far between.

The canoes were dugouts made from hollowed out cedar logs, which was the best material available at the time. They ranged in size from the small one or two-man vessels, probably the pickup trucks of that time, to huge war canoes, capable of carrying 30 or 40 men and covering long distances. The Haidas of the Queen Charlotte Islands in British Columbia travelled as far south as the Fraser River and Puget Sound on their raiding parties, primarily to take captives for slaves. In 1857, the Tlingits of Kake, Alaska, then Russian territory, went all the way to Whidbey Island, Washington, to kill Isaac Ebey, a United States Customs collector, in revenge for the killing of one of their chiefs. So, much before the advent of the first Europeans, there was waterborne traffic along the Inside Passage.

The first Europeans, the Russians, Spanish, English and French, all came in various types of sailing vessels, mostly armed war ships. They were very small ships by today's standards. The *Santiago* that Quadra, the most famous and diligent of the Spanish explorers, and his crew sailed from the naval base at San Blas, Mexico, to Alaska on a voyage of several months, was only 36 feet long. Following in the wakes of these early explorers, the sailing ships of the fur traders, who were after the skins of the sea otters, were also relatively small.

The first steamship brought to the coast was the Hudson's Bay Company *Beaver* which arrived in 1836. She was a side-wheeler, 70 feet long, and used to bring supplies to the company's posts and to return with furs. She also took the occasional passenger looking for transportation north. The only other means of *public transportation* at that time was in your own skiff or small sailboat, or, which was often the case, by hiring some natives and their cedar canoe. As late as 1846, most local communication at Victoria with the *outside world*, primarily Puget Sound, was transported by way of a large cedar canoe acquired by the Hudson's Bay Company from the Haidas of the Queen Charlotte Islands. It carried mail and passengers as well as some freight.

In 1853, the Hudson's Bay Company brought the steamer *Otter* around Cape Horn to British Columbia to assist the *Beaver* on her rounds. The *Otter*, 122 feet long, was a screw, or propeller driven steamer, and a great advancement over the *Beaver*. Both were great improvements over the sailing ships, especially for traversing the narrow waterways of the Inside Passage.

As the Puget Sound region started to be settled in the 1850's and 1860's, enterprising mariners started offering transportation services around the sound in small paddle wheel steamers. As this fleet of small ships grew, it became known as *The Mosquito Fleet*.

The first heavy traffic on the Inside Passage was in response to the Fraser River Gold Rush of 1858 which, the first summer, brought between 25,000 to 30,000 gold seekers to the area. Most came to Victoria on paddle wheel steamers or sailing ships from San Francisco. Others arrived, by the same means, to Port Townsend and Bellingham, two United States ports. The next problem was to cross Georgia Strait to the mouth of the Fraser River, and then proceed up the river by some means. At first, canoes, rafts, rowboats and small sailboats were the only craft available. Enterprising American shippers brought small steamers up from California and Puget Sound. By the end of 1858, it was possible to go to the gold fields by taking a steamer from Victoria all of the way across the Strait of Georgia and up the Fraser River to Fort Hope, the head of transportation at that time.

The Hudson's Bay Company steamers provided the only coastal service in British Columbia as well as competing with others for the Fraser River traffic. In 1883, the Hudson's Bay Company fleet was combined with the competing Pioneer Line to form the Canadian Pacific Navigation Company, with the Hudson's Bay Company retaining controlling interest. In 1901, the Canadian Pacific Railway Company gained control of the Canadian Pacific Navigation Company. In 1903, the name was changed to the British Columbia Coast Service of the Canadian Pacific Railway Company. This company with its numerous *Princess* ships, dominated the passenger traffic of the Inside Passage, from Seattle, Victoria and Vancouver to Prince Rupert, Juneau and Skagway until the outbreak of World War II. At first, the only major competition came from two sources: the Union Steamship Company of British Columbia, Ltd. which specialized in servicing the small ports, lumber camps, canneries and mines up the coast from Vancouver, and the Puget Sound Navigation Company which provided service between Seattle and Victoria.

The history of the Union Steamship Company is very interesting and is well covered by Gerald Rushton in his excellent book, *Whistle Up the Inlet* (see bibliography). While the Canadian Pacific Navigation Company, The Canadian Pacific Railway, The Canadian National Railway, and the Alaska Steamship Company ran the *express through service* up the coast, the Union Steamship Company ran the *local service*. They continued this service for 70 years, employing, at various times, more than 50 different ships, all of them relatively small, enabling them to get into the numerous small harbors that they serviced. In times when fog, rain, or snow restricted visibility, and lacking today's radar, the captains, knowing the speed of sound, used an echo returning from a blast of the ship's whistle to determine their distance from shoreline. It is remarkable that in all of the years that the Union Steamship Company provided these coastal services, there were only two instances where lives were lost by accidents. Only six lives were lost out of the thousands of passengers carried, although there were many groundings and several ships were lost. However, through the years, the larger faster steamers of the lines providing service to Alaska lost numerous ships and hundreds of lives during their operations.

The gold rush to Juneau in 1880-81 resulted in the establishment of regular, frequent transportation from Seattle, Victoria, Vancouver, Portland and San Francisco.

The Klondike Gold Rush of 1896-1899 changed the transportation pattern of the Inside Passage, by opening it up in its entirety for the first time. Every available vessel was pressed into service to transport the gold seekers, along with tons of freight, that sought passage to Dyea, Skagway and Nome. After the boom was over, traffic dropped off. People continued to take passage to Alaska, if only for a summer cruise or visit.

As previously mentioned, after 1900 the Canadian Pacific Navigation Company emerged as the dominant carrier until World War II intervened. Their large fast ships named " *Princesses*, covered the waters from Puget Sound to Skagway. The Inside Passage routes were only a small part of the Canadian Pacific Railway's seagoing ambitions.

A few weeks after the first train arrived on May 23, 1887, in what was becoming the city of Vancouver, a ship, the *Abyssinia* which the Canadian Pacific had chartered along with two sister ships, the *Parthia* and the *Batavia*, arrived from Yokohama, Japan. They carried the first trans-Pacific mail and the first shipment of silk, as well as tea, which were transferred to the railroad to speed them on their way to England. With the already established fleet of passenger vessels from England to Halifax and Montreal, and the new transcontinental railroad, the Canadian Pacific's empire stretched from Europe to the Orient. In 1891, the first of the famous Canadian Pacific *Empresses*, the *Empress of India* was placed in service along with her sisters, *Empress of Japan* and *Empress of China*. They were beautiful white ships with graceful clipper bows and overhanging sterns, and provided swift first class service across the Pacific.

In addition to the Union Steamship Company, the Canadian Pacific was challenged by an American firm, the Alaska Steamship Company. Even before the completion of the Grand Trunk Pacific Railway to Prince Rupert, British Columbia in April, 1914, the Grand Trunk Pacific Coast Steamship, Ltd. was formed, and also began to compete with the Canadian Pacific. Their vessels were named *Princes*, the *Prince Rupert* and *Prince George*, a pretty obvious takeoff from the *Princesses*. The vessels of these three lines continued to compete and provide fast deluxe service along the Inside Passage until the advent of World War II in 1939.

After World War II, great changes were made in the transportation system. Public transportation systems took over passenger carrying on both short and long distances. The Washington State Ferry System was organized to carry both passengers and vehicles in the Puget Sound area, replacing the former privately owned ships. The biggest share of passenger traffic was to and from the west side of the sound to Seattle and nearby communities. The same thing took place in British Columbia, when the British Columbia Ferries took over from private interests, primarily the Canadian Pacific Railway. In Alaska, the Alaska Marine Highway System began service in 1963 between Southeast Alaskan cities and Prince Rupert, British Columbia, where they connected with existing railway and highway systems. In 1967, service was extended to Seattle. In 1989, Bellingham, Washington replaced Seattle as the southern terminus.

Before World War II, ships of the two Canadian lines, The Canadian Pacific Railway and the Canadian National Railway, dominated the cruise ship trade. However, they were pressed into wartime service, and only a few survived. In the 1970's, a great boom began occurring in this industry. Today, numerous cruise ships ply these waters in the spring, summer, and fall months. These huge ships, sailing mostly from Vancouver, with some from Seattle, visit ports along the route, such as Petersburg, Ketchikan, and Juneau before reaching their destinations of Skagway and Glacier Bay in Alaska. They do not provide *transportation* in the conventional definition, but primarily entertainment, food, and opportunities for scenic views for the passengers, the great majority of whom are aboard for a *round trip*. New and larger cruise ships appear every year, and the number of passengers increases accordingly.

The handling of freight has shifted from the steamships that formerly operated, to tugs which tow barges and to large container ships. Freight can be stowed in huge containers that are hauled to the port on semitrailers for direct loading and unloading onto the ship. These are privately owned operations.

TRANSPORTATION BY RAIL

Transcontinental railroads of the United States and Canada were very important, not only in the development of the northwest coast, but also to the Inside Passage. Before the advent of these railways, the only access to the Pacific Northwest was by ship, first sail, and later steam powered. The long, arduous and costly route from Europe or the East Coast of the United States was around South America, including tempestuous and dangerous Cape Horn at the south end of the continent.

The completion of the first transcontinental railroad, the Union Pacific-Central Pacific to Oakland and San Francisco in 1869, created an easier, faster and less expensive route to the Pacific Coast. San Francisco became the port used by all passengers and also for much of the freight going north. As other rails reached the coast farther north, other seaports came into being. The Northern Pacific Railroad reached Portland, Oregon, in 1883, and traffic began flowing along that route. In 1888 the Northern Pacific Railroad was completed to Tacoma, Washington, the first rail connection to the Inside Passage itself. The Great Northern Railroad reached Seattle, Washington, in 1893, and Seattle soon outgrew Tacoma, becoming the main seaport of the Pacific Northwest.

In Canada, the first transcontinental railroad, the Canadian Pacific Railway, was completed to Port Moody, British Columbia, on Burrard Inlet, in November, 1885. The stage was set for the development of Vancouver, farther down Burrard Inlet where the first train arrived on May 23, 1887.

The Grand Trunk Pacific Railway was completed to Prince Rupert, British Columbia, in April, 1914, giving Canada another Pacific port, 500 miles closer to Asian and Alaskan markets than Vancouver and other Pacific ports. Each of the important seaports on the Pacific

Coast came into being when it was given a rail connection to the east and to the rest of the continent.

The importance of the railways to the development of the entire Inside Passage cannot be overemphasized. It is certain that the Klondike Gold Rush of 1896-99 would have had only a fraction of the gold seekers who actually were involved if cheap rail transportation to the west coast had not been available. The new railways, eagerly seeking passengers, competed by cutting their fares to ridiculously low figures, encouraging the flood of would-be miners.

TRANSPORTATION BY AIR

The proliferation of air transportation that occurred all over the world after World War II also came to the Inside Passage. Today, airlines carry the majority of the travellers as well as a good share of freight. The first scheduled airline service to Alaska began in 1940, by Pan American Airways System using Sikorsky flying boats from Seattle to Ketchikan and Juneau. In British Columbia, the Canadian Pacific Airlines, owned by the ever present Canadian Pacific Railway, became the dominant carrier, with Queen Charlotte Airlines, an independent airline, providing competition. Seattle, Tacoma and Vancouver have developed large international airports with service connections to the entire globe. In the late 1990's, the air carrier which provides the majority of the air services to Alaska from Seattle is Alaska Airlines, and, in British Columbia, Canadian Airlines International and Air B.C. provide service between Prince Rupert, Port Hardy, Vancouver and Victoria.

Anyone travelling along the Inside Passage is soon aware of another type of air transport found all along it, from Seattle to Skagway. That is the so-called "bush plane", mounted on floats. These float planes range in size from the single engine, four passenger Cessna 180's and eight passenger DeHaviland Beavers, to the twin engine Grumman Goose and DeHaviland Twin Otter, the latter carrying 20 passengers. Capable of landing on lakes and rivers as well as on salt water, they provide service to logging and mining camps, sportsfishing lodges, marinas, and communities, both large and small, along the coast. They are owned and operated by a variety of small operators based in towns and cities along the Inside Passage.

SHIPWRECKS

The Inside Passage is known as one of the most treacherous and difficult waterways to navigate in the world, so it should not be a surprise to find that it has a long history of shipwrecks. Many of the early wrecks occurred not in the passage itself, but in the approaches to it, in the Strait of Juan de Fuca, around Cape Flattery, on the south side of the west entrance to the Strait, and on the southwest shore of Vancouver Island, on the north side of the entrance. In the days of sailing ships, when most of them came into Puget Sound to pick up lumber or coal, many crashed on Vancouver Island shores during frequent winter storms or fog banks. Strong winter currents, of which the captains were not aware, often carried them past the entrance to the Strait.

One of the worst marine casualties in the Strait of Juan de Fuca was to a passenger steamer, the *Pacific*, on November 4, 1875, when she was struck by the sailing ship *Orpheus* in fog near Cape Flattery, and sank within a few minutes. Out of the 277 people aboard the *Pacific*, 275 perished. The captain of the *Orpheus* did not believe that the *Pacific* had been seriously damaged and continued on his way. He missed the entrance to the Strait, as did many other skippers, and piled the *Orpheus* up on Cape Beale, Vancouver Island the next day.

Another tragedy occurred in the Strait of Juan de Fuca when the Black Ball Line steamer *Clallam* foundered at the east end of the strait on a trip from Seattle to Victoria in a big storm on January 9, 1904. Fifty five of the passengers and crew died. About 30 were rescued by two tug boats before she sank.

There were many wrecks in Puget Sound itself as ship traffic increased. Most were without large losses of lives. On November 18, 1906, however, the passenger steamer *Dix* foundered off Alki Point in West Seattle with the loss of 39 lives. Many of the shipwrecks in Puget Sound and the Strait of Juan de Fuca were the result of collisions due to heavier traffic, and the frequent periods of poor visibility that occur in these waters.

The 500 miles of the Inside Passage that run through British Columbia have seen hundreds of ships and small boats wrecked along its length. Its shores have many underwater rocks just under the surface waiting for the unsuspecting mariner. Strong currents occur in many of the narrow passages, and add to the potential hazards.

Some of the strongest currents are in Seymour Narrows, about seven miles north of Campbell River on Vancouver Island, right on the main shipping lane to the north. The rapids attain velocities as great as 16 knots. To make matters worse, Ripple Rock was in the center of Seymour Narrows, within ten feet of the surface at low water, greatly obstructing the passage and increasing the turbulence of the waters. Ripple Rock was the most deadly hazard in the entire length of the

Inside Passage, and claimed its first recorded victim, the United States Navy ship *USS Saranac* in 1875. Between 1875 and 1958, two dozen ocean going ships and barges were either lost or damaged by striking Ripple Rock, with 114 lives lost in the process. Hundreds of smaller vessels were also lost or damaged.

At 9:31 a.m. on April 7, 1958, the rock was partially removed by the largest nonnuclear man-made explosion to that date, when 2.75 million pounds of high strength explosives were detonated and 400,000 tons of rock were shot sky high. Through the years, all other attempts had failed to remove the rock. The final, successful attempt required drilling a shaft 572 feet deep on Maud Island and driving a 2,400 foot tunnel under the waterway to locations under the two peaks of Ripple Rock. Shafts were then dug up into the offending rocks, and smaller tunnels drilled into them. These small tunnels were then packed with the high explosives. The entire process took two years and employed between 40 and 80 men. The results were even better than expected because about seven to ten feet more of the rock was removed than was anticipated, giving a least depth of about 50 feet at low tide. The tidal currents still run as strong as ever through Seymour Narrows, and create hazardous conditions for small craft, but the danger from Ripple Rock is gone forever.

Seymour Narrows had not claimed its last victim, however, as the cruise ship *Sundancer*, bound for Alaska in June of 1984, was hurled onto the rocks of Maud Island and severely damaged. The captain took her into nearby Menzies Bay and tied to the wharf of the pulp mill, enabling her crew and 800 passengers to be saved. However, the ship was so badly damaged that she sank at the wharf.

One of the earliest reported shipwrecks in Southeast Alaska was a Russian warship, the frigate *Neva*, that foundered on the rocks at Cape Edgecumbe on Kruzof Island about 20 miles west of Sitka, on January 9, 1813. She was bringing supplies from Siberia, and had a long history in Alaskan waters. She was the warship that had aided Governor Baranof when he defeated the natives and reestablished Sitka after it had been taken from the Russians by the Tlingits in the massacre of 1802. A few of the Russians survived the shipwreck, but 33 lives were lost as well as the cargo and the ship.

During the Klondike Gold Rush, the little steamer *Al-ki* departed Seattle on July 19, 1857 grossly overloaded with both passengers and cargo. The supply of shipping could not begin to meet the demand, and unscrupulous operators began using anything that would float, including old ships that had been condemned, or even abandoned on a beach. When the problems created by these substandard ships were compounded by manning with inexperienced crews unfamiliar with the northern waters, noncompliance with safety regulations, and overloading to the maximum degree possible, it is a wonder that there were not more wrecks and fatalities than those which did occur. The worst accident was when the ship *Clara Nevada* having ignored the laws prohibiting carrying passengers when the cargo contained explosives, blew up in Lynn Canal, between Juneau and Skagway, only a few miles short of her destination. All 65 people aboard were lost as well as the ship and cargo.

The Gold Rush did open the Inside Passage for regular service for its entire length for the first time. In February, 1899, there were 41 regular ships operating out of San Francisco harbor alone, bound for Alaska. One unintended benefit from all of the shipwrecks was the location of many hitherto uncharted hazards, and their inclusion on newly published charts.

The next major shipwreck in Alaskan waters occurred on August 15, 1901, to the *Islander*, the pride of the Canadian Pacific Navigation Company, the finest ship on the Alaskan run, and advertised as *unsinkable* due to her several watertight compartments. Sounds familiar, doesn't it?

After departing Juneau about midnight, with 181 persons aboard, including the crew of 61, she ran into fog and plowed into an iceberg at full speed. The ensuing gash in her plates opened several of the watertight compartments to the sea. Most of the passengers and crew were able to get into life boats before she sank, but 41 lives were lost. Ships did not yet carry radios, so no other ships came to her aid. Some of the survivors started walking to Juneau, and got help from steamers at the Treadwell Mine. The *Islander* went down in 300 feet of water, but was successfully raised 32 years later as the result of an inaccurate report which stated that large amounts of gold were aboard. About $40,000 worth of gold was all that was found, not enough to pay for the salvage operations, and she was scrapped for her metal.

On September 20, 1908, the 262 foot long sailing vessel, the *Star of Bengal*, crashed on the rocks of Helen Point on Coronation Island, 100 miles southwest of Wrangell, Alaska. She was bound for San Francisco with a cargo of canned salmon and 133 persons aboard. Most of the passengers were Oriental cannery workers returning after the end of the canning season. Only 22 people survived. With the loss of 111 lives, it was one of the worst shipwrecks in Alaska.

The *SS Mariposa*, one of the best and fastest ships of the Alaska Steamship Company, ran ashore on Strait Island, off Point Baker, Alaska, 40 miles west of Wrangell, on November 18, 1917, and sank with her cargo of copper ore and canned salmon. All of her 265 passengers had been taken off safely.

The most deadly shipwreck of the entire Inside Passage occurred on October 24, 1918, when the Canadian Pacific passenger liner the *Princess Sophia* ran onto Vanderbilt Reef in Lynn Canal, Alaska, 40 miles north of Juneau. She was carrying 268 passengers and a crew of 75. Her captain originally thought that she was in no immediate danger because the ship had double bulkheads and a double bottom. He may have thought that she could be refloated, as had been a sister ship, the *Princess Mary*, when she had grounded on nearby Sentinel Island eight years earlier. Due to rough seas, the captain decided to wait for better weather before evacuating the passengers, even though several ships had responded to the SOS and were standing by. The weather worsened as darkness fell and the would-be rescuers were forced to seek shelter. During the night the storm blew the *Princess Sophia* off the reef and she sank. Her last message was "For God's sake, come. We are sinking." When the ships returned to Vanderbilt Reef the next morning the only sign of the *Sophia* was the tips of her masts. All 343 of her passengers and crew were drowned. The lighthouse tender, *Cedar*, was one of the vessels responding to the SOS. On board she had a lighted buoy to replace the unlit can buoy which was in place when the *Sophia* struck.

Two more large Canadian passenger liners were lost in the years after World War II, but only one life was lost. On September 22, 1945, the Canadian National Railway ship, the *Prince George*, ran aground in a fog near Ketchikan, Alaska and was virtually destroyed by fire when a fuel tank exploded. One seaman was killed when trapped in the engine room. The ship was beached and eventually refloated in 1949, towed to Seattle, and sold for scrap.

The four million dollar Canadian Pacific Railway's ship, the *Princess Kathleen*, was lost on September 7, 1952, when she ran onto the rocks of Lena Point, on the mainland 18 miles north of Juneau. The 425 passengers and crew were evacuated without any casualties, but when the tide came in, the ship slipped off the rocks, and sank, a total loss.

One of the most interesting shipwreck histories is that of the steamer *Ohio*. Her bow section is still clearly visible, rising out of the water in Carter Bay, British Columbia, just off Finlayson Channel, about 120 miles south of Prince Rupert. She was a large American ship, 335 feet long. Before she came to the west coast, she had served on the Trans-Atlantic run. She departed Seattle for Alaska on August 24, 1909, with 135 passengers and crew and a cargo of steel railroad rails. On the 28th of August, while making her way up Finlayson Channel in a heavy rainstorm, darkness fell. At 1:00 a.m., while travelling at full speed, she struck an uncharted rock. The blow ripped open her side, allowing water to enter. The captain knew that she would not stay afloat for long, and looked for a place to beach his ship. The rocky shores plunged straight down into deep water, but Carter Bay, about five miles away, had some shallow water near its river mouth. He headed there as the ship began to fill and sink. She was beached in Carter Bay and, in half an hour, sank to the bottom with the bow section remaining above water. As the ship was abandoned, the passengers reached the nearby shore in life boats. The crew took a lifeboat to the nearest settlement, the Butedale Cannery, and a vessel came to rescue the passengers. The

SOS signal that was sent was not picked up because the steep, high mountains interfered with radio transmission. Four lives were lost, including that of the radio man who struck his head on some floating wreckage as he dove from the ship. He and two other crew members had remained with the captain. Subsequent storms have torn off the ship's wheel house, but the bow still remains, well above even high tides. Salvagers removed the cargo, engines and propeller, but no effort was made to recover the ship. As has happened in many other cases, the rock that sank the *Ohio* is now named after her. The latest charts still show *Ohio Rock*.

The BC Ferry and Alaska Ferry transfer passengers and vehicles.

CHAPTER TEN

EFFECTS OF WORLD WAR II
ON THE INSIDE PASSAGE

World War II impact was great on the Inside Passage, and all of Alaska, as well as the entire world. In September 1939, at the beginning of the war in Europe, only 524 military personnel were stationed in the whole Territory of Alaska; of these a large number were operating the telegraph and cable service. By July, 1943, the number had expanded to 152,000. Starting in 1940, the Navy developed bases at Sitka, Kodiak and Dutch Harbor. Later the Army arrived in Anchorage, Fairbanks and the Aleutians. In early 1941, a tremendous movement of cargo began. More than 300 military installations were built in Alaska before the war was over, at a cost of over $350 million.

Relatively few people lived in Alaska prior to the war. A 1939 census listed 75,524 residents, almost half of them Natives. More than 20 percent of the total population lived in five Southeast Alaska towns. Juneau, the capital and largest city in Alaska had 5,720 people. Ketchikan was number two, and Anchorage and Fairbanks were three and four. Salmon fishing was the mainstay of the territory's economy.

The inaction on the part of Congress in attending to the possibility of foreign attacks on Alaska was not because there had not been voices demanding that something be done. One of the loudest voices was that of Brigadier General William (Billy) Mitchell of the Army Air Service in the 1920's. Mitchell was a firm believer in the future importance of air power. He was familiar with Alaska, having served there as a Lieutenant in the Army Signal Corps in 1901, surveying, on snowshoes and dogsled, and overseeing the building of the telegraph line between Valdez and Eagle. He predicted that someday unfriendly forces might try to use Alaska as an invasion route into North America. He also foresaw that Alaska was "one of the most strategic places in the world" on the trans-polar route between the Orient, Europe and eastern United States. He was correct, because today many United States, European and Asian airlines stop in Anchorage to refuel their trans-polar flights.

In May, 1940, with World War II having been well under way in Europe since the previous September, Congress finally awoke and appropriated money for Army bases in Anchorage and coastal defenses at Kodiak and Dutch Harbor in the Aleutians. Troops, civilian construction crews, and equipment poured into Alaska, most of it shipped up the Inside Passage, and then across the Gulf of Alaska, dwarfing even the movements of men and freight of the 1897-99 Yukon Gold Rush. Seattle again was the main shipping port, along with neighboring Tacoma. They were soon swamped by the sheer volume of shipping involved, especially after Pearl Harbor and the entrance of the United States into the fray. The fortification of Alaska became a joint United States-Canada affair, and Canadian ports and railroads were utilized to provide additional capacity for shipping. Prince Rupert, in particular, became very important as the Canadian National Railway serving it provided additional rail capacity, and its location was 500 miles closer to Alaska. Eventually 5,000 American troops were based in Prince Rupert to handle the volume of men and material passing through the port.

Although the Southeast Alaska airfields and seaplane bases were operational and troops had begun to arrive at Anchorage, Kodiak and Dutch Harbor, Alaska was still poorly defended when America declared war on Japan after the December 7th, 1941, bombing of Pearl Harbor. The 11th Air Force had only six medium bombers and 12 pursuit planes, or fighters. The Navy had some old World War I destroyers and a gunboat "Charleston", along with six seaplanes and the seaplane tender, "Gillis", out of Washington. Ammunition, fuel and oil were in short supply. The Army ordered more planes to Alaska, but getting them there wasn't easy. It was the middle of winter, the air crews were inexperienced, and the route was across the northern Canadian wilderness, from Edmonton via incomplete, poorly marked airfields at Fort St. John, and Fort Nelson in British Columbia, Watson Lake and Whitehorse in the Yukon Territory, and Northway and Big Delta in Alaska to Fairbanks, Alaska. There were many problems and they showed that there was a need for an overland supply route to Alaska. The Army had been attempting for some time to have a road built as an alternate supply route if the water routes should be denied them by enemy action. Early in 1942, an agreement with Canada gave the Americans the route to build a 1,500 mile highway, the ALCAN, as it was known in those days, from Dawson Creek, British Columbia, to Fairbanks, Alaska. It is now called the Alaska Highway. The route of the

105

new road nearly followed the one that the United States Army was using for its planes, tying together the remote airfields, and providing men and equipment to improve them. Eighty percent, or 1,200 miles of the ALCAN crossed Canadian territory, and 20 percent, or 300 miles was in Alaska. The agreement between the two countries stated that the United States would survey and construct the road, and maintain the completed highway until "termination of the present war and for six months thereafter, unless the Government of Canada prefers to assume responsibility at an earlier date for the maintenance of so much of it as lies in Canada." Work was begun on March of 1942, and the *"pioneer"* road was completed on November 20, 1942, ready for emergency use only at first, at a cost of $150 million. Work continued on the highway for another year. After the war, on April 1, 1946, the Canadian section of the ALCAN highway was turned over to Canada.

The majority of the air traffic through the small airfields located along the ALCAN consisted of aircraft transferred to Russia under the American "Lend Lease" Program that was originally enacted in March, 1941, as a method of assisting Britain in the war against Nazi Germany. After Germany invaded Russia, the aid was extended to Russia. The transfer of planes began in September, 1942, and more than 7,900 aircraft, bombers and fighters, flew through Fairbanks, where they were turned over to the Russians, along this route to Siberia during the war.

Although it has often been overlooked in recounting the various battles of World War II, Alaska actually experienced military combat, the first on American soil since the Civil War and the Indian Campaigns. In June, 1942, the Japanese bombed Dutch Harbor, and invaded the Aleutian Islands of Attu and Kiska. Soon after, a small United States Navy fleet defeated a more powerful Japanese armada in the Komandorski Islands west of the Aleutians, cutting off attempts to resupply the occupied islands. Through early 1943, American air and naval forces bombed and shelled Kiska and Attu.

On May 11, 1943, American forces landed on Attu in a dense fog that made air and naval support of the invasion almost impossible. The battle for Attu was a difficult one, even though the Japanese were greatly outnumbered, they refused to surrender, preferring death. When the battle was over, at the end of May, 1943, 2,350 Japanese were dead and only 29 were taken prisoner. American losses were 540 killed and 1,148 wounded, one of the most costly battles in the Pacific.

Kiska was the next and last target for Allied troops, and bombing by the 11th Air Force intensified after the capture of Attu. On August 15, 1943, a landing force of 30,000 Americans and 5,300 Canadians went ashore. Three battleships, two cruisers, 19 destroyers and 70 additional naval vessels represented the United States Navy, and air power consisted of 24 heavy bombers, 44 medium bombers, 28 dive bombers, 12 patrol bombers and 60 fighters; plenty of power. A special force consisting of, part of the American 10th Mountain Infantry Division and Canadians trained in winter mountaineering, and the Alaska Scouts, all Alaska residents, went ashore a day before the main force to test the Japanese resistance. In the dense fog, the soldiers mistook each other for the enemy and fired, 17 Americans and four Canadians were killed. Booby traps also took some lives. Seventy-one men died and 14 were wounded when a destroyer hit an enemy mine. When the situation calmed down, it became obvious that there were no Japanese left on Kiska. The Japanese had evacuated 5,183 men on submarines, six destroyers, two cruisers and their landing craft by slipping through the American blockade. Before leaving, about 500 Japanese were lost during the numerous bombing raids. Thus ended the Aleutian campaign, the Japanese took their troops back to Japan, leaving nearly all of their equipment behind them.

Canada, a member of the British Commonwealth, declared war on Germany on September 10, 1939, nine days after Great Britain, and ten days after Hitler's attack on Poland on September 1, 1939. Canada made a big contribution to the Allied efforts in World War II, not only in men but in war materials. Though she made large contributions to air and land forces, her greatest contribution was in sea power. At the end of the war she had one of the largest navies in the world, measured by the number of ships, not total tonnage, for most of the ships were relatively small, destroyers, corvettes, frigates and mine sweepers. The strength of the Royal Canadian Navy grew from 5,000 men to over 100,000 during the war. The naval forces were concentrated in the north Atlantic, primarily in the escorting of convoys to and from Great Britain.

Though Canada's presence in the North Atlantic was considerable, her Pacific Coast defenses were minimal, as they had been in World War I. There was very little danger of a land invasion, because of the country's best defense, the ruggedness of the terrain.

After the Japanese air raid at Pearl Harbor on December 7, 1941 and the entry of the United States into World War II, the Canadians realized that their Pacific coastline needed protection, especially after the Japanese attacked the Aleutian Islands in Alaska in the first week of June, 1942, and the Estavan Point Lighthouse on the west coast of Vancouver Island was shelled by a Japanese submarine on June 20, 1942. The submarine fired about 25 six-inch shells, but did no damage to the lighthouse or its staff.

The Canadians built coast defense gun emplacements at the entrances to their harbors as early as 1939, the beginning of the war in Europe. With a 600-mile long coast line to protect, the defenses were limited to the harbors, except for a most interesting fortification on Yorke Island at the east end of Johnstone Strait, between Vancouver Island and the mainland. The strait is only three miles wide and all traffic on the Inside Passage must go through it, so the guns effectively blocked any enemy ships, though none ever showed up.

As previously mentioned, the bulk of the ships of the Royal Canadian Navy were on convoy duty in the North Atlantic, leaving only a small number to defend the Pacific Coast. To supplement this weak fleet, the Canadians organized the Fishermans' Reserve Service, composed of about 40 commercial fishing boats, mostly large wooden purse seiners, and their experienced crews to establish a full time reconnaissance patrol of the entire British Columbia coast. This patrol performed until the end of the war. The boats were skippered and manned by reserve personnel, but were directed by regular naval authorities out of Victoria and Prince Rupert.

American coastal defenses of the entrance to Puget Sound were at Port Townsend on the south side of the Strait of Juan de Fuca and on Whidbey Island on the north side. The guns were removed after the war, but the empty gun enclosures, are located at the sites of Washington State Parks, open to the public, and interesting to visit.

The main Canadian emphasis on defense of their west coast was based on air power, and a series of air bases were built along the coast. Four large airfields were built on Vancouver Island, making it, as someone said, "an unsinkable aircraft carrier." These bases were at Sidney, north of Victoria, at Comox, at Tofino on the west coast of the island, and at Port Hardy on the north end. Comox is still used as a Canadian Forces airbase, and all four of the fields are used by commercial aircraft today. In the north an airfield was built at Sandspit in the Queen Charlotte Islands; it is in commercial use today. In addition, seaplane bases were built at Shearwater, near Bella Bella on the north coast, and at Ucluelet on the west coast of Vancouver Island. PBY long range patrol bombers flew out of these seaplane bases.

As noted previously, the Aleutian campaign was a joint United States-Canadian effort, with 5,300 Canadians going ashore at Kiska, along with the 30,000 Americans.

The war also had a considerable effect on the economies of the communities along the Inside Passage. In the Puget Sound area, port facilities were enlarged at both Seattle and Tacoma to handle the tremendous amount of material being shipped to Alaska, as well as troops. The ship building industry also boomed, building both naval and commercial ships. A new industry for the area, aircraft manufacturing, primarily by Boeing, arrived on the scene, and is still of great importance today. The demand for building materials increased the output of the timber industry. Military bases were established as exemplified by Fort Lewis, near Tacoma, and Ault Field, Whidbey Island's Naval Air Station. The natural result of all of this economic growth was, of course, a corresponding increase in the population of the entire Puget Sound region.

To the north, in Canada, Vancouver and Victoria both experienced a boom in shipbuilding for both the navy and the merchant marine, as well as some aircraft manufacturing on Sea Island, the site of today's Vancouver International Airport.

The volume of shipping through Vancouver Harbour also soared, much of it an overflow from the United States ports.

In Alaska, most of the military installations were not built along the Inside Passage, but father north in the Aleutians and the center of the state. In the Alaska "*Panhandle*" a naval air station was built at Sitka, to protect the southwest coast and an army air field was built on Annette Island, 40 miles southwest of Ketchikan. The field at Sitka is still used by the United States Coast Guard and commercial aircraft, but the Annette Island airfield has seen little use since an airstrip was built in 1973 on Gravina Island, across Tongass Narrows from Ketchikan.

At Skagway, the Army took over the operation of the White Pass and Yukon Railroad to Whitehorse in the Yukon Territory of Canada, to provide men and equipment to build the ALCAN highway. Twelve thousand troops landed in Skagway, a town of 600. The Army also built a pipeline from Skagway to Whitehorse to provide fuel for the project, as well as a backup route for aircraft fuel in case the enemy denied them the sea route for tanker traffic.

At Haines, the Army built a highway to Whitehorse and the new ALCAN highway to provide an alternate route to the narrow gauge White Pass and Yukon Railroad.

Most of the ships carrying men and cargoes to the main theaters of operations in Alaska passed through the Inside Passage on their way north and had a positive effect on the communities of Southeast Alaska.

Shortly after the Japanese attack on Pearl Harbor, and the subsequent entry of the United States into World War II, the United States and Canadian governments carried out some of the most reprehensible acts they have ever committed when they arrested all people of Japanese descent living in the areas adjacent to their Pacific coastlines and herded them into concentration camps for the duration of the war. This was done without due process of law and violated the rights of these people, who were, in the majority, either United States or Canadian born, or naturalized citizens of their respective countries. They were only allowed a few hours to gather up their children and what property they could carry with them. All of the remaining assets were sold at prices well below their fair market values, if not looted by their former neighbors.

The reasons for these acts were said to be fear that these people would either sabotage the war effort, or aid Japan in the event of an invasion. References were made to the actions of the so-called "*Fifth Column*" in the Spanish Civil War of the 1930's, but it was largely a purely racist act.

EPILOGUE

What is the state of the Inside Passage today, over 200 years after it was first explored by Captain George Vancouver? One might say that it has a split personality, because of the way population is distributed along its length. The southern end, 160 air miles from Olympia, Washington to Vancouver, British Columbia is heavily populated along the corridor of land between the Cascade, or Coast Range Mountains and the salt water. Immediately north of Vancouver the mountains push their way west right to the salt water, and form the eastern side of the Inside Passage all the way to Skagway, and "*civilization*" ceases.

The British Columbia coast extends northwest over 500 miles to the Alaska border, and the only community of any size on the mainland is Prince Rupert, with a population of 17,000, just 40 miles south of the border. It is actually on Kaien Island, just adjacent to the mainland. The only roads that penetrate the mountains to the salt water in the 500 mile stretch of coastline are one from Williams Lake in the interior to Bella Coola on North Bentinck Arm, the road from Terrace to Kitimat at the head of Douglas Channel and one to Stewart at the head of Portland Canal, 120 miles north of Prince Rupert. At Prince Rupert, the huge Skeena River breaches the mountains and the Yellowhead Highway, a paved road, and the Canadian National Railroad follow it, coming west from Prince George, British Columbia, and Edmonton and Jasper in Alberta. This stretch of the coast, between Vancouver and Prince Rupert, has been referred to by some as the "*deserted coast*", because it has fewer inhabitants now than any time since the retreat of the glaciers, 10,000 years ago. At one time, the native population exceeded the total of today, prior to being decimated by disease about 200 years ago.

When the salmon canneries were operating at full blast they brought thousands of people to the coast, if only on a seasonal basis;

but the canneries are all gone now, consolidated in a few big canneries in Prince Rupert and Vancouver. The lumber camps used to employ large numbers, but mechanization has greatly reduced those numbers. Most of the former mining camps have depleted their mineral deposits, and are abandoned. Sports fishing camps and fish farming, or aquaculture, have begun to turn the tide in the last 25 years, but the net result is a much diminished population.

The Alaskan section of the Inside Passage locally referred to as the *"Southeast"* has also been subject to large fluctuations in its population, first the great reduction in the Native population by diseases, then the boom and bust periods of the three great gold rushes, and lastly the boom during World War II. It is still very sparsely populated outside the seven towns or cities that it contains. About 69,000 people live along the Alaskan section of the Inside Passage according to the 1990 United States census. Seventy percent live in the seven major communities of Juneau (29,755), Ketchikan (15,082), Sitka (9,194), Petersburg (3,350), Wrangell (2,400), Haines (1,363) and Skagway (767). More than 20% are native, Tlingit, Haida, and Tsimshian.

The capitals of the three political subdivisions through which the Inside Passage runs all lie on the passage. Olympia, Washington state's capital, is the southern terminus of the passage, with a population of 34,000; Victoria, British Columbia's capital, is 100 miles to the north, on the southern tip of Vancouver Island, with a population of 66,000; and Juneau, Alaska's capital, with a population of 29,000 is just 80 miles south of Skagway, the north end of the Inside Passage.

When Alaska became a state in 1959 the governmental role of Juneau increased. Juneau's site has drawbacks as the location of a state capital: first, it is certainly not a central location; and second it has no roads connecting it to the rest of the state because of the mountainous terrain. It can only be reached by air or water. Because of these shortcomings, the citizens of Alaska voted in 1974 to move the capital away from Juneau to a site between Anchorage and Fairbanks. The proposal stated that Anchorage could not be the new capital because it was felt that the non-Anchorage voters would not approve of that location, and would defeat the proposal. In 1976 the new site was selected near the village of Willow, about 65 road miles north of Anchorage. In November, 1982, after the voters got the estimated cost of making the move, they defeated a funding proposal, and Juneau continues to be the state capital for the foreseeable future. Today, government; state, federal and local, continues to occupy an estimated one half of the local industry.

The two large population centers at the south end of the Inside Passage, Seattle and Vancouver, each have a population of about 500,000, with two to three times that in their metropolitan areas. They are both large transportation hubs, with aircraft, ships and trains arriving from and departing for destinations all around the world. Each of them has become a truly cosmopolitan community with several universities, large and small, symphony orchestras, excellent opera companies and thriving legitimate theaters. Keeping up with the current trends, each of them has a full complement of major league professional sports teams. Both cities have hosted large World Fairs, Seattle in 1962 and Vancouver in 1986; the latter to celebrate the 100th anniversary of the completion of the Canadian Pacific Railway to Vancouver.

The industry that has fueled the economy of Puget Sound during World War II and ever since has been the aircraft industry, represented by Boeing, the largest aircraft manufacturer in the world. In recent years another giant has appeared on the scene, Microsoft, a computer software firm based in Bellevue, a Seattle suburb.

The chief industry in Vancouver, British Columbia, in recent years has been the construction industry, both commercial and residential. Construction cranes have been a familiar sight as one skyscraper after another rose in the downtown area. This building boom was fueled largely by money brought in by new Asian immigrants from Hong Kong departing before the turnover of the colony to China in 1997. Vancouver was the favorite relocation site for these immigrants. By the mid-1990's ethnic Chinese made up one fourth of Vancouver's population. A July 23, 1997 article in the Wall Street Journal stated in its headline, "For Vancouver the Party is Over". This was based on a reversal of the flow of immigrants from Hong Kong, and their capital that began the previous year, when China signalled that they would not curtail economic freedom after the takeover. Suddenly investment opportunities in China became much more attractive, with less *red tape* and lower taxes. According to this article, the feeling in Vancouver is not one of alarm, but rather that the flow of capital will resume, if not from Hong Kong, then from other Asian sources.

Tourism has become one of the most important industries in all of the communities that border the Inside Passage, and continues to become more important with each year that passes. This is particularly true of the cruise ship facet of the tourist industry. Since about 1975 the numbers of ships and passengers cruising up and down the waters of the Inside Passage to Alaska each summer has grown at an incredible pace. In the summer of 1997 there were 42 different ships employed, half of them capable of carrying from 1,000 to 2,400 passengers per trip. These big ships not only increase in numbers each year, but the new ones are ever larger. The majority of these large cruise ships are owned by two dominant operators, Princess Cruises and Holland America Westours, with thirteen vessels between them. Many of the remaining cruise ships are much smaller, with passenger capacities of 100 to 200. These smaller ships have become very popular in the '90's, not everyone thinks that "bigger is better". The smaller ships can get into places that are denied to the huge ships, just because of their size.

In 1997 it is estimated that over 400,000 passengers will take cruises along the Inside Passage.

Nearly all these cruise ships depart from Vancouver instead of Seattle, despite the fact that most of the passengers are United States citizens. This is due to an antiquated piece of United States legislation called the Passenger Services Act, passed in 1886. This act states that foreign-flagged vessels, those registered in foreign ports, taking on passengers at a United States Port must stop at a foreign port before returning these passengers to a United States port. Only three cruise lines in the world sail under the United States flag, and they are very small in size.

The reason that ships are not registered in the United States, is the higher costs of operating them. The much higher wages required by the United States maritime unions account for nearly all of these increased costs. In the spring of 1997, a bill was introduced in the United States Senate rewriting a portion of this act to allow these foreign ships to sail between United States ports. It will probably not be any more successful than earlier attempts have been to change this act.

Currently most of the passengers fly into Seattle and are taken to their ships in Vancouver by bus or plane. The demand for these cruises grows every year, witness the ever increasing number of passengers.

In addition to the cruise ships plying the waters of the Inside Passage, the ferries of the Alaska Marine Highway, operating the Alaska State Ferry System, carry about 200,000 additional passengers. The Alaskan System connects five of the major cities in southeast Alaska to each other, as well as to Prince Rupert, British Columbia, where highway and rail connections are available and to Bellingham, Washington, ninety miles north of Seattle. At the northern end the Alaskan System services the ports of Skagway and Haines, where there is highway access to the Alaska Highway. The British Columbia ferry system's coastal service runs between Prince Rupert and Port Hardy, on the north end of Vancouver Island.

If the cruise ships and ferries carry around 600,000 passengers each year, that is about six times as many each year as made this trip during the entire 1897-99 Klondike Gold Rush. These ships customarily visit one of the ports and disembark their passengers each day, then reload and head for a new port the next day. The economic effect of having 5,000 or 6,000 tourists, new ones each day, all summer long, in the communities of Ketchikan, Sitka, Juneau and Skagway, is considerable to say the least.

There are a couple of interesting aspects of this new major "industry" for the Inside Passage. First it appears to be a "renewable" or "non-depleting" resource, at least so far, and secondly it has a very low impact on the environment. This was not true of previous "industries"; furs, mining, timber and fishing all exploited and eventually depleted the resources on which they depended.

  The drawback is that the benefits are limited to only a few communities, those where the cruise ships or ferries dock. All things considered, however, it would appear that the future looks bright for this fabulous waterway and its residents.

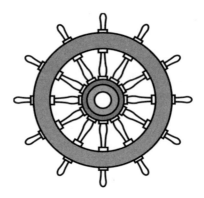

Tourism has become a vital industry. The number of cruise ships touring the Inside Passage is multiplying every year.

BIBLIOGRAPHY

Akrigg, G.P.V. and Helen B., *British Columbia Chronicle, 1778-1846*.
Discovery Press, Vancouver, British Columbia, 1975.

Akrigg, G.P.V. and Helen B., *British Columbia Chronicle, l847-l871*.
Discovery Press, Vancouver, British Columbia, 1977.

Alaska Geographic, Vol. 5, No. 2, *Southeast Alaska's Panhandle*.
Alaska Geographic Society, Anchorage, Alaska, 1978.

Alaska Geographic, Vol. 11, No. 4, *Alaska Steam, The Alaska Steam
ship Company*.
Alaska Geographic Society, Anchorage, Alaska, 1984.

Alaska Geographic, Vol. 14, No. 2, *South/Southeast Alaska*.
Alaska Geographic Society, Anchorage, Alaska, 1987.

Alaska Geographic, Vol. 20, No. 2, *Southeast Alaska*.
Alaska Geographic Society, Anchorage, Alaska, 1993.

Alaska Geographic, Vol. 23, No. 2, *Native Cultures in Alaska*.
Alaska Geographic Society, Anchorage, Alaska, 1996.

Alaska Geographic, Vol. 24, No. 1, *Alaska's Southern Panhandle*.
Alaska Geographic Society, Anchorage, Alaska, 1997.

Anderson, Bern, *The Life and Voyages of Captain George Vancouver,
Surveyor of the Sea*.
University of Toronto Press, 1960.

Avery, Mary W., *Washington, A History of the Evergreen State*.
University of Washington Press, Seattle, Washington, 1961.

Bancroft, Hubert H., Vol. XXXI, *History of Washington, Idaho and
Montana, 1845-1889*.
The History Company Publishers, San Francisco, 1890.

Bancroft, Hubert H., Vol. XXXII, *History of British Columbia, 1792-
1887*.
The History Company Publishers, San Francisco, 1890.

Bancroft, Hubert H., Vol. XXXIII, *History of Alaska, 1845-1889*.
The History Company Publishers, San Francisco, 1890.

Berton, Pierre, Klondike, *The Last Great Gold Rush, 1896-1899.*
McClelland and Stewart, Inc., Toronto, Ontario, Canada, 1987.

Browning, Robert J., *Fisheries of the North Pacific.*
Alaska Northwest Publishing Company, Anchorage, Alaska, 1974.

Campbell, Kenneth, *North Coast Odyssey.*
Sono Nis Press, Victoria, British Columbia, 1993.

Chevigny, Hector, *Lord of Alaska, Baranov and the Russian Adventure.*
The Viking Press, New York, New York, 1944.

Chevigny, Hector, *Russian America, The Great Alaskan Adventure, 1741-1867.*
Binfort and Mort, Portland, Oregon, 1965.

Gibbs, Jim, *Disaster Log of Ships.*
Superior Publishing Company, Seattle, Washington, 1971.

Halliday, Jan and Chehak, Gail, *Native Peoples of the Northwest.*
Sasquatch Books, Seattle, Washington, 1996.

Hilson, Stephen E., *Exploring Puget Sound and British Columbia, Olympia to Queen Charlotte Sound.*
Van Winkle Publishing Company, Holland, Michigan, 1975.
Reprinted Evergreen Publishing Company,
Seattle, Washington, 1997.

Inglis, Robert, *Spain and the North Pacific Coast.*
Vancouver Maritime Museum Society, Vancouver, British Columbia, 1992.

McNaught, Kenneth, *The Penguin History of Canada.*
Penguin Books, Ltd., London, England, 1988.

Morgan, Murray, Puget's Sound, *A Narrative of Early Tacoma and the Southern Sound.*
University of Washington Press, Seattle and London, 1979.

Newman, Peter C., *Caesars of the Wilderness, Company of Adventurers, Vol. II.*
Penguin Books Canada, Ltd., Markham, Ontario, Canada, 1988.

Nicholson, George, *Vancouver Island's West Coast, 1762-1962*.
    George Nicholson, Victoria, British Columbia, 1965.

Ormsby, Margaret A., *British Columbia, A History*.
    Macmillan of Canada, 1958.

Raincoast Chronicles #4.
    Harbour Publishing, Madeira Park, British Columbia, 1976.

Raincoast Chronicles #7.
    Historical Society, Madeira Park, British Columbia.

Rogers, Fred, *Shipwrecks of British Columbia*.
    Douglas and McIntyre, Vancouver/Toronto, 1973.

Rushton, Gerald A., *Whistle Up the Inlet*.
    J. J. Douglas, Ltd., Vancouver, 1974.

Sale, Roger, *Seattle, Past to Present*.
    University of Washington Press, Seattle, Washington, 1976.

The Wall Street Journal.
    New York, New York, July 23, 1997.

Woodcock, George, *British Columbia, A History of the Province*.
    Douglas and McIntyre, Vancouver/Toronto, 1990.

PHOTO CREDITS

Hugo Anderson

Rachel Anderson

Campbell River Chamber of Commerce

Gwen Cole

Virginia Kimmett

Prince Rupert Chamber of Commerce

Stephanie Satter

Linda Schreiber

Jack Schreiber

INDEX

118

121

123